Meeting the Needs
of Your Most Able Pupils:

MUSIC

.023

.WN

Other titles in the series

Meeting the Needs of Your Most Able Pupils: Art
Kim Earle
1 84312 331 2

Meeting the Needs of Your Most Able Pupils: Design and Technology
Louise T. Davies
1 84312 330 4

Meeting the Needs of Your Most Able Pupils: Physical Education and Sport
David Morley and Richard Bailey
1 84312 334 7

Meeting the Needs
of Your Most Able Pupils:
MUSIC

Jonathan Savage

 David Fulton Publishers

David Fulton Publishers Ltd
The Chiswick Centre, 414 Chiswick High Road, London W4 5TF

www.fultonpublishers.co.uk
www.onestopeducation.co.uk

David Fulton Publishers is a division of Granada Learning Limited, part of ITV plc.

Note: the right of Jonathan Savage to be identified as the author of this work has been
asserted by him in accordance with the Copyright, Designs and Patents Act 1988.

Copyright © Jonathan Savage 2006

British Library Cataloguing in Publication data
A catalogue record for this book is available from the British Library.

ISBN: 1 84312 347 9

10 9 8 7 6 5 4 3 2 1

Series production editor: Andrew Welsh
Typeset by Servis Filmsetting Ltd, Manchester
Printed and bound in Great Britain

Contents

Foreword

It is inconceivable that a school can claim to be taking forward the personalisation agenda seriously without having a robust approach to gifted and talented education.

(Rt Hon. Jacqui Smith MP, Minister of State, Schools and 14–19 Learners, January 2006)

Effective schools provide an appropriate education for all pupils. They focus on the needs of individuals and design their offer to take account of the needs of the main recognised groups. Gifted and talented pupils are now a recognised group within each school. For a school to be effective it must plan its provision for these pupils, identify those who will benefit and monitor the effectiveness of their offer through its impact on the learning outcomes of pupils. This formalises the position of gifted and talented education and ensures that the needs of the most able are not overlooked.

Since 2000 we have begun to see the impact of a clear focus on the needs of gifted and talented pupils in the education system. The Qualifications and Curriculum Authority (QCA) and the National Strategies have begun to focus on this group and to provide materials and training to support teachers. The Office for Standards in Education (Ofsted) takes their needs into account when assessing the performance of a school and the government has established the National Academy for Gifted and Talented Youth (NAGTY) to steer this agenda.

NAGTY's role is to drive forward improvements in gifted and talented education by developing a national, government-supported catalyst that can provide leadership and support for professionals working in this field. To achieve this, it works with students, parents, teachers, education professionals, specialist providers, universities and business. Children and young people are at the heart of the Academy's mission. NAGTY aims to ensure that all children and young people, regardless of background, have access to the formal and informal learning opportunities they need to help them convert their potential into high achievement.

Gifted education in England is very much part of the overall education system and deeply embedded in it. The English model of gifted and talented education is a description of this approach and the rationale for it. Provision is rooted in day-to-day classroom provision and enhanced by additional, more advanced opportunities offered both within school and outside of it. Giftedness is a term used to describe children or adults who have the *capacity* to achieve high levels of expertise or performance. Giftedness in childhood could be described as 'expertise in its development phase'. Therefore, the education of gifted and talented pupils should focus on expertise development. Giftedness is developmental and is developed through individuals gaining access to appropriate opportunities and support. Performance levels are directly affected by availability of appropriate opportunities and support. Direct intervention with individuals can help reverse the effect of socioeconomic disadvantage or other lack of support.

Provision for gifted children should be made in ordinary schools as part of the day-to-day educational offer. This core provision should be supplemented by access to enhanced opportunities offered both within and beyond the school. Schools should themselves be diverse and distinctive in nature and so offer specific opportunities to develop certain aptitudes and parents should be seen as co-educators with a key role in supporting learning.

This series of books is a welcome addition to the literature base. It aims to help teachers make the English model a reality. In this model every teacher needs to be a teacher of the gifted. They need to understand how to teach the gifted and talented and have both the confidence and the skills to make that a reality on a day-to-day basis. While there are generic aspects to provision for gifted and talented pupils, the majority of classroom provision is subject-based and so it is through a subject approach that most teachers will consider the needs of their most able pupils. This series of books aims to help teachers within the subject domains to become more effective teachers of the gifted and talented pupils in their class. It builds on the emerging frameworks supplied by DfES, NAGTY and the government agencies and interprets them within a subject-specific context.

Without doubt this series of books will be a considerable help to both individual teachers and to schools seeking to improve provision for their gifted and talented children and young people.

PROFESSOR DEBORAH EYRE
Director, NAGTY

Acknowledgements

My thanks go to the following people who have contributed case studies, ideas, teaching materials and extended pieces of writing for inclusion in this book and the accompanying CD:

Mrs Pat Calcutt, head of music, Bedford High School, for a pupil case study in Chapter 4.

Mr Andy Cope, head of music, Leek Specialist Technology School, for pupil case studies in Chapter 4.

Ms Emma Coulthard, Nottingham City LEA, for policy materials in Chapter 2.

Mrs Janet Cunningham, curriculum manager for the performing arts and arts college coordinator, St Michael's Church of England High School, for a departmental case study in Chapter 6.

Mr David Evans, head of music, Tottington High School, for examples of assessment practice in Chapter 4.

Mr Will Evans, senior lecturer in music education, Manchester Metropolitan University, for a case study on baseline assessment in Chapter 2.

Dr Martin Fautley, senior lecturer in music education, University of Central England, for writing on assessment (Chapter 4, pp. 80–88) and on creativity and learning styles (Chapter 5, pp. 101–114).

Ms Beverley Herron Pembec (in conjunction with Wigan LEA), for all the documents relating to work at Kingsdown School.

Ms Jo Lord, head of music, Middleton Technology College, for a pupil case study in Chapter 4.

Mr Richard Lord, head of music, Flixton Girls' High School, for pupil case studies in Chapter 4.

Mr Kenton Mann, managing director, Music Unlimited, for case studies in Chapter 5.

Mrs Jane Petrie, music adviser, Wigan LEA, for many examples of policy and practice included in Chapter 2 and on the accompanying CD.

Ms Janet Redwood, head of music, Cheadle Hulme College, for the preparation of Appendix 2.2.

Mrs Judy Waters, head of music and head of talent, Longdendale Community Language College, for the preparation of the case study concluding Chapter 4 and many materials included on the accompanying CD.

Mr Ian Yates, MMU trainee teacher 2004–2005, for examples of assessment practice in Chapter 4.

And to all the MMU postgraduate students, subject mentors, and my colleague Will – whose constant ideas, enthusiasm and experience keep me going. A big THANK YOU to you all.

Contributors to the series

About the author

Jonathan Savage is a senior lecturer in music education at the Institute of Education, Manchester Metropolitan University. Until 2001 he was head of music at Debenham High School, an 11–16 comprehensive school in Suffolk. He is a co-author of a new resource introducing computer game sound design to the Key Stage 3 curriculum (www.sound2game.net) and managing director of UCan.tv (www.ucan.tv), a company specialising in the production of educational software and hardware. When not doing all of this, he is busy parenting four very musically talented children!

Series editor

Gwen Goodhew's many and varied roles within the field of gifted and talented education have included school G&T coordinator, director of Wirral Able Children Centre, Knowsley Excellence in Cities (EiC) G&T coordinator, member of the DfES G&T Advisory Group, teacher trainer and consultant. She has written and edited numerous reports and articles on the subject and co-authored *Providing for Able Children* with Linda Evans.

Other authors in the series

Art

Kim Earle is a former secondary head of art and design and is currently an able pupils and arts consultant for St Helens. She has been a member of DfES steering groups, is an Artsmark validator, a subject editor for G&TWISE and is a practising designer jeweller and enameller.

Design and Technology

During the writing of the D&T book **Louise T. Davies** was a part-time subject adviser for design and technology at the QCA (Qualifications and Curriculum Authority), and part of the KS3 National Strategy team for the D&T programme. She has authored over 40 D&T books and award-winning multimedia resources. She is currently deputy chief executive of the Design and Technology Association.

Physical Education and Sport

David Morley has taught physical education in a number of secondary schools. He is currently senior lecturer in physical education at Leeds Metropolitan University and the director of the national DfES-funded 'Development in PE' project which is part of the Gifted and Talented strand of the PE, School Sport and Club Links (PESSCL) project. He is also a member of the team responsible for developing resources for national Multi-skill Clubs and is the founder and director of the Carnegie Regional Multi-skill Camp held at Leeds Met Carnegie.

Richard Bailey is a professor of pedagogy at Roehampton University, having previously worked at Reading and Leeds Metropolitan University, and at Canterbury Christ Church University where he was director of the Centre for Physical Education Research. He is a well-known author and speaker on physical education, sport and education.

Contents of the CD

The CD accompanying this book may be used by the purchasing individual/organisation only. It contains files which may be amended to suit particular situations, or individual learning needs, and printed out for use by the purchaser.

Highlights from the CD

What to include in a gifted and talented policy (3)

Kingsdown High School G&T policy (5)

Lord Williams's School G&T policy (6)

Departmental approaches to the able student (7)

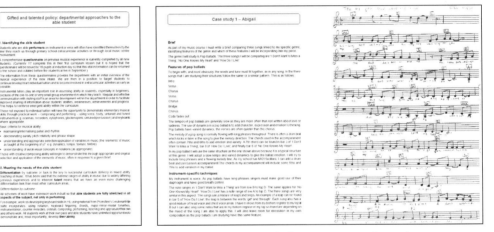

Composition case study (12) with recordings (13–15)

Identifying the gifted and talented pupil cohort, including detailed methods and processes (11)

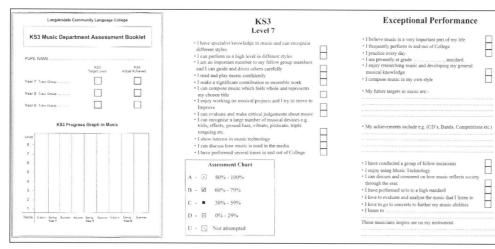

Longdendale High School assessment booklet (24)

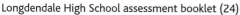

Questioning gifted and talented pupils (33)

Music department mentoring policy (34)

Role of the talent mentor (35)

Differentiation in the music department (36)

Special needs in the performing arts (37)

Sample talent certificates (40)

Introduction

Who should use this book?

This book is for all teachers of music working with Key Stage 3 and Key Stage 4 pupils. It will be relevant to teachers working within the full spectrum of schools, from highly selective establishments to comprehensive and secondary modern schools as well as some special schools. Its overall objective is to provide a practical resource that heads of department, gifted and talented coordinators and classroom teachers can use to develop a coherent approach to provision for their musically talented pupils.

Why is it needed?

School populations differ greatly and pupils considered very able in one setting might not stand out in another. Nevertheless, whatever the general level of ability within a school, there has been a tendency to plan and provide for the middle range, to modify for those who are struggling and to leave the most able to 'get on with it'. This has meant that the most able have:

- not been sufficiently challenged and stimulated

- often underachieved

- been unaware of what they might be capable of achieving

- not had high enough ambitions and aspirations

- sometimes become disaffected.

How will this book help teachers?

This book and its accompanying CD, through its combination of practical ideas, materials for photocopying or downloading, and case studies of individual pupils, departmental policy and practice, will:

- help teachers of music to focus on the top 5–10% of the ability range in their particular school and to find ways of providing for these pupils, both within and beyond the classroom

- equip them with strategies and ideas to support exceptionally able pupils, i.e. those in the top 5% nationally.

Terminology

Since there is confusion about the meaning of the words 'gifted' and 'talented', the terms 'more able', 'most able' and 'exceptionally able' will generally be used in this series.

When 'gifted' and 'talented' are used, the definitions provided by the Department for Education and Skills (DfES) in its Excellence in Cities programme will apply. That is:

- **gifted** pupils are the most academically able in a school. This ability might be general or specific to a particular subject area, such as mathematics.

- **talented** pupils are those with high ability or potential in art, music, performing arts or sport.

The two groups together should form 5–10% of any school population. In this book, the term 'musically talented pupils' has been agreed on by a consultative group of experienced heads of music departments in high schools across the North West of England and university staff. It will be used to describe pupils who are talented in music. By this, we mean all pupils who are talented and, although the government may struggle with this idea, also those pupils who are gifted musicians (see Chapter 3 for further discussion of this point).

There are, of course, some pupils who are both gifted and talented across the curriculum subjects. Examples that come to mind are the budding physicist who plays the violin to a high standard in his spare time, or the pupil with high general academic ability who plays for the area football team.

This book is part of a series dealing with providing challenge for the most able secondary age pupils in a range of subjects. It is likely that some of the books in the series might also contain ideas that would be relevant to teachers of music.

CHAPTER 1

Our more able pupils – the national scene

- Making good provision for the more able – what's in it for schools?
- National initiatives since 1997
- LEA responsibilities to more able pupils
- School Ofsted inspections and more able pupils
- Some tools to support inspection and school development plans
- Other general support for teachers and parents of more able pupils

The purpose of this first chapter is to place the subject-specific content of all that follows into the more general national and school framework. We know it is easier to understand what needs to be done at departmental level if there is an appreciation of the context in which discussions are held and decisions are made.

The debate about whether to make special provision for the most able pupils in secondary schools ran its course during the last decade of the twentieth century. Explicit provision to meet their learning needs is now considered neither elitist nor a luxury. As part of an inclusive educational policy, these pupils must have the same chances as others to develop their potential to the full. But even for teachers who are not convinced by the inclusion argument, there is a much more pragmatic reason for meeting the needs of able pupils. Quite simply, it is something that all teachers are now required to do, not an optional extra.

> All schools should seek to create an atmosphere in which to excel is not only acceptable but desirable.
>
> (*Excellence in Schools* – DfEE 1997)

> High achievement is determined by the school's commitment to inclusion and the steps it takes to ensure that every pupil does as well as possible.
> (*Handbook for Inspecting Secondary Schools* – Ofsted 2003a)

A few years ago, efforts to raise standards in schools concentrated on getting as many pupils as possible over the Level 5 hurdle at the end of Key Stage 3 and over the five A*–C grades hurdle at GCSE. Resources were pumped into borderline pupils and the most able were not, on the whole, considered a cause for concern. The situation has changed dramatically in the last five years with schools being expected to set targets for A*s and As and to show added value by helping pupils entering the school with high SATs scores to achieve Levels 7 and beyond, if supporting data suggests that that is what they are capable of. Early recognition of high potential and the setting of curricular targets are at last addressing the lack of progress demonstrated by many able pupils in Year 7 and more attention is being paid to creating a climate in which learning can flourish. Nevertheless, there is a push for even more support for the most able through the promotion of personalised learning.

> The goal is that five years from now: gifted and talented students progress in line with their ability rather than their age; schools inform parents about tailored provision in an annual school profile; curricula include a gifted and talented dimension and at 14–19 there is more stretch and differentiation at the top end, so no matter what your talent it will be engaged; and the effect of poverty on achievement is reduced, because support for high-ability students from poorer backgrounds enables them to thrive.
>
> (Speech at the National Academy for Gifted and Talented Youth – David Miliband, Minister of State for School Standards, May 2004)

It is hoped that this book, with the others in this series, will help to accelerate these changes.

Making good provision for the most able – what's in it for schools?

Schools and/or subject departments often approach provision for the most able pupils with some reluctance because they imagine a lot of extra work for very little reward. In fact, the rewards of providing for these pupils are substantial:

- It can be very stimulating to the subject specialist to explore ways of developing approaches with enthusiastic and able students.

  > Taking a serious look at what I should expect from the most able and then at how I should teach them has given my teaching a new lease of life. I feel so sorry for youngsters who were taught by me 10 years ago. They must have been bored beyond belief. But then, to be quite honest, so was I.
  >
  > (Science teacher)

- Offering opportunities to tackle work in a more challenging manner often interests pupils whose abilities have gone unnoticed because they have not been motivated by a bland educational diet.

  > Some of the others were invited to an after-school maths club. When I heard what they were doing, it sounded so interesting that I asked the

maths teacher if I could go too. She was a bit doubtful at first because I have messed about a lot but she agreed to take me on trial. I'm one of her star pupils now and she reckons I'll easily get an A*. I still find some of the lessons really slow and boring but I don't mess around – well, not too much.

(Year 10 boy)

- When pupils are engaged by the work they are doing, motivation, attainment and discipline improve.

  You don't need to be gifted to work out that the work we do is much more interesting and exciting. It's made others want to be like us.

  (Comment from a student involved in an extension programme for the most able)

- Schools that are identified as very good schools by Ofsted generally have good provision for their most able students.

  If you are willing to deal effectively with the needs of able pupils you will raise the achievement of all pupils.

  (Mike Tomlinson, former director of Ofsted)

- The same is true of individual departments in secondary schools. All those considered to be very good have spent time developing a sound working approach that meets the needs of their most able pupils.

  The department creates a positive atmosphere by its organisation, display and the way that students are valued. Learning is generally very good and often excellent throughout the school. The teachers' high expectations permeate the atmosphere and are a significant factor in raising achievement. These expectations are reflected in the curriculum which has depth and students are able and expected to experience difficult problems in all year groups.

  (Mathematics department, Hamstead Hall School, Birmingham; Ofsted 2003)

National initiatives since 1997

Since 1997, when the then Department for Education and Employment (DfEE) set up its Gifted and Talented Advisory Group, many initiatives designed to raise aspirations and levels of achievement have been targeted on the most able, especially in secondary schools. Currently, a three-pronged approach is in place, with:

1. special programmes, including Excellence in Cities, Excellence Clusters and Aimhigher, for areas of the country where educational standards in secondary schools are lowest

2. resources for teachers and pupils throughout the country, such as the National Academy for Gifted and Talented Youth, gifted and talented summer schools, World Class Tests, National Curriculum Online and the G&TWISE website

3. regional support, which is currently confined to GATE A, in London.

1. Special programmes

Excellence in Cities

In an attempt to deal with the chronic underachievement of able pupils in inner city areas, Excellence in Cities (EiC) was launched in 1999. This is a very ambitious, well-funded programme with many different strands. It initially concentrated on secondary age pupils but work has been extended into the primary sector in many areas. 'Provision for the Gifted and Talented' is one of the strands.

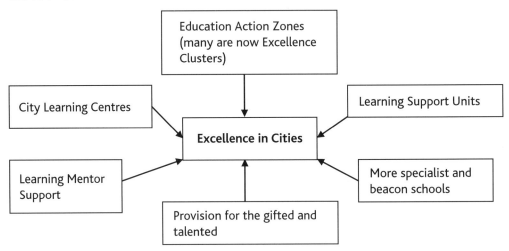

Strands in the Excellence in Cities initiative

EiC schools are expected to:

- develop a whole-school policy for their most able pupils

- appoint a gifted and talented coordinator with sufficient time to fulfil the role

- send the coordinator on a national training programme run by Oxford Brookes University

- identify 5–10% of pupils in each year group as their gifted and talented cohort, the gifted being the academically able and the talented being those with latent or obvious ability in PE, sport, music, art or the performing arts

- provide an appropriate programme of work both within the school day and beyond

- set 'aspirational' targets both for the gifted and talented cohort and for individual pupils

- work with other schools in a 'cluster' to provide further support for these pupils

- work with other agencies, such as Aimhigher, universities, businesses and private-sector schools, to enhance provision and opportunities for these pupils.

The influence of Excellence in Cities has stretched far beyond the areas where it is in place. There are a number of reasons for this:

- Partnership (LEA) gifted and talented coordinators set up regional support groups. These groups worked to raise awareness of the needs of these pupils and their teachers. One of the most successful is the Transpennine Group, which operates from Liverpool across to Hull. Early meetings concentrated on interpreting Department for Education and Skills (DfES) directives but later the group invited universities, support organisations, publishers and successful practitioners to share ideas with them. They also began to run activities for pupils across all the EiC partnerships involved. By constantly feeding back information from the meetings to the DfES, it began to have some influence on policy. Teachers and advisers outside EiC areas have adopted similar models and the DfES is now funding regional support groups that include both EiC and non-EiC areas.

- Publishers have responded to demand from gifted and talented coordinators and are producing more materials, both books and software, that challenge the most able.

- Some LEAs have worked with Oxford Brookes University to extend their coordinator training into non-EiC areas.

- **The requirements of EiC schools have come to be regarded as a blueprint for all secondary schools.** The DfES guidance for EiC schools is available for all schools at www.standards.dfes.gov.uk/giftedandtalented.

Excellence Clusters
Although EiC was set up initially in the main urban conurbations, other hotspots of underachievement and poverty have since been identified and Excellence Clusters have been established. For example, Ellesmere Port, Crewe and Barrow-in-Furness are pockets of deprivation, with major social problems and significant underachievement, in otherwise affluent areas. Excellence Clusters have been established in these three places and measures are being taken to improve provision for the most able pupils.

Aimhigher
There have been a number of changes in EiC over the years. One of the most recent is that, in secondary schools, the EiC programme now supports the most able between the ages of 11 and 14, but from 14 to 19 their needs are met through Aimhigher, another initiative of the DfES. Its remit is to widen participation in UK higher education, particularly among students from groups that do not have a tradition of going to university, such as ethnic minorities, the

disabled and those from poorer homes. Support for these pupils begins while they are still in school and includes:

- activities in schools and colleges to encourage them and raise their aspirations

- extra money to universities to enable them to provide summer schools and outreach work with pupils

- The Young People's Publicity Campaign providing information and advice to those from disadvantaged backgrounds

- financial support for students through 26,000 Opportunity Bursaries worth £2,000 each over three years for young people.

The Aimhigher website is at www.aimhigher.ac.uk.

2. Resources for teachers and pupils throughout the country

National Academy for Gifted and Talented Youth

Government initiatives for the most able pupils have not been confined to those in deprived areas. In 2002, the National Academy for Gifted and Talented Youth was established at Warwick University. Its brief is to offer support to the most able 5% of the school population and to their teachers and parents, and it is doing this in a number of ways.

The National Academy for Gifted and Talented Youth		
Student Academy • Summer schools, including link-ups with the Center for Talented Youth (CTY) in the USA • Outreach courses in a wide range of subjects at universities and other venues across the country • Online activities – currently maths, classics, ethics and philosophy	**Professional Academy** • Continuing professional development (CPD) for teachers • A PGCE+ programme for trainee teachers • Ambassador School Programme to disseminate good practice amongst schools	**Expertise Centre** • Leading research in gifted and talented education

Bursaries are available for pupils from low-income families so that they are not denied access to the activities. The Academy's website is at www.nagty.ac.uk.

Gifted and talented summer schools

Each LEA is provided with money to run a number of summer schools (dependent on the size of the authority) for the most able pupils in Years 6–9. The approach to the selection and management of these schools differs from area to area. For example, some authorities organise them centrally while others allow schools to bid to run one of the summer schools. The main aim obviously is to challenge and stimulate these pupils but the DfES also hopes that:

- the summer schools will encourage teachers and advisers to adopt innovative teaching approaches
- teachers will continue to monitor these pupils over time
- where Year 6 pupils are involved, it will make secondary teachers aware of what they can achieve and raise their expectations of Year 7 pupils.

More can be found out about these summer schools at: www.standards.dfes.gov.uk/giftedandtalented/. Unfortunately, direct funding from the DfES for summer schools ceased in 2005.

World Class Tests

These have been introduced by the Qualifications and Curriculum Authority (QCA) to allow schools to judge the performance of their most able pupils against national and international standards. Tests are currently available for 9- and 13-year-olds in mathematics and problem solving. Some schools have found that the problem solving tests are effective at identifying able underachievers in maths and science. The website, at www.worldclassarena.org.uk, contains sample questions so that teachers, parents and pupils themselves can assess the tests' suitability for particular pupils or groups of pupils.

National Curriculum Online

The National Curriculum Online website, administered by QCA, provides general guidance on all aspects of the National Curriculum but also has a substantial section on general and subject-specific issues relating to gifted and talented education, including identification strategies, case studies, management and units of work. The website is at www.nc.uk.net/gt.

G&TWISE

The G&TWISE website has recently replaced the one called Xcalibre. It links to recommended resources for gifted and talented pupils, checked by professionally qualified subject editors, in all subjects and at all Key Stages. It is part-funded by the Gifted and Talented Education Unit of the DfES. The website is at www2.teachernet.gov.uk/gat/.

3. Regional support

At this stage, regional support is confined to GATE A, a branch of London Challenge. Four London EiC partnerships have collaborated with universities, cultural centres and professional bodies to develop a coordinated approach to supporting the most able pupils throughout the region.

Central to this is the MLE or Managed Learning Environment, which provides pupils with interactive learning materials. Some key features of this include:

- video conferencing and online alerts for specific groups of users
- online assignments and tests

- course calendars and linked personal calendars

- personal study records.

GATE A provides five 'Student Learning Pathways' so that the approach can be matched to a student's stage of development and needs. There are subject, themed and cross-curricular skills-based pathways as well as one directed at Aimhigher students, and one for work-related learning. The initiative also strives to support the parents and carers of more able pupils. The website is at www. londongt.org.

The initiatives discussed above do not include the many subject specific developments, such as those from QCA, that have taken place during this period. These will be dealt with in later chapters.

LEA responsibilities to more able pupils

Schools and departments should not be shy of approaching their LEA for help when developing their more able pupil provision. Local authorities, as well as schools, are expected to support more able pupils and schools can and should turn to them for support and advice.

The notes from Ofsted on LEA Link Inspection published in December 2003 state that the main tasks of LEAs, with regard to offering support to schools for gifted and talented pupils, are:

- to provide guidance to schools in meeting pupils' needs

- to identify schools which need particular help and to ensure that this is provided effectively

- where appropriate, to support initiatives across the LEA, such as gifted and talented summer schools, Excellence in Cities, Excellence Clusters and helping pupils to access resources such as the National Academy for Gifted and Talented Youth

- to support individual pupils with particular talents in order that they make progress

- to learn lessons from Excellence in Cities areas.

After a period when many LEAs did very little to support these pupils in a systematic manner, the climate has now changed and many have taken measures such as:

- producing gifted and talented guidelines for schools

- running continuing professional development (CPD) programmes, sometimes with the help of Oxford Brookes University, which provide training for EiC gifted and talented coordinators

- encouraging federations of local schools to work together to make additional provision for the most able

- setting up masterclasses and advanced learning centres

- identifying good practice in schools and disseminating this to other schools in the authority.

Ofsted – expectations of secondary schools

The most able must be seen to have as many opportunities for development as other pupils. Poor, unchallenging teaching or an ideology that confuses equality of opportunity with levelling down must not hinder their progress. The environment for learning should be one in which it is safe to be clever or to excel.

Throughout the new Ofsted *Handbook for Inspecting Secondary Schools* (2003a), there are both direct and indirect references to schools' responsibilities to their most able pupils. Wherever the phrase 'all pupils should . . .' appears in this handbook, teachers need to ask themselves not only how this applies to pupils with special educational needs (SEN) and other disadvantaged groups but also how this applies to their most able pupils.

A summary of some of the more important points relating to more able pupils from this handbook is included in Appendix 1.1, where page numbers are provided so that teachers can find out more.

Some tools to support inspection and school development plans

In light of the above, teachers might find the Pre-Ofsted checklist (on the next page) and the National Quality Standards in Gifted and Talented Education (Appendix 1.2) helpful either when preparing for Ofsted or when looking into developing this area of work as part of the school development plan. More about national quality standards in gifted and talented education can be found at www.standards.dfes.gov.uk/giftedandtalented/strategyandstrands.

It is important to remember that:

- the development of provision for the more able should be firmly enmeshed with other curricular and pastoral strategies and should fit in to the overall school philosophy

- classroom practice should match school and departmental policy.

	Pre-Ofsted able pupil checklist	✓
1.	Does the school have a policy for its most able pupils?	
2.	Is there a school coordinator for the most able?	
3.	Is there someone in each department with whom the coordinator can liaise?	
4.	Are there identification strategies in place that are understood by all?	
5.	Do these strategies identify both academic ability and talent in specific areas of the curriculum?	
6.	Does the balance of the most able cohort match the school profile in terms of gender, ethnicity and social class?	
7.	Do pupils' achievements match their potential taking into account the school's performance data and other evidence?	
8.	Is negative stereotyping of the most able challenged?	
9.	Do teachers support the most able with: – high expectations?	
10.	– the employment of a wide range of teaching styles?	
11.	– a suitable pace?	
12	– extension and enrichment activities?	
13.	– the selection of suitable resources?	
14.	Does the school's organisation of pupils into groups and sets take account of the needs of these pupils?	
15.	Does the school have an appropriate curriculum for the most able?	
16.	Do pupils have access to any of the following: learning mentors; study support; out-of-school activities; masterclasses; specialists; resources in other schools and colleges?	
17.	Are senior managers alert to the need to monitor and track the progress of the most able?	
18.	Is suitable training for staff arranged when the need arises?	
19.	Do senior managers take action when the needs of the most able are not being met?	
20.	Are the most able pupils positive about the education and support they receive in the school?	
21.	Are parents content with school provision?	

Other general support for teachers and parents of more able pupils

Two organisations which must be included when there is any mention of support for more able pupils, their teachers and parents are NACE and NAGC.

NACE

The National Association for Able Children in Education, or NACE as it is generally known, is primarily a support organisation for teaching professionals. It has many publications on the education of more able pupils, many of them produced in association with David Fulton Publishers. Its Challenge Award has been particularly well received. Conferences are regularly held around the country and training can be provided at school, LEA or regional level. It can also provide consultancy tailored to the individual needs of schools. The Association's website is at www.nace.co.uk.

NAGC

The focus of the National Association for Gifted Children is primarily on the children themselves although it does offer support to parents and teachers as well. It can offer:

- branches throughout the country where children with similar interests or abilities can meet at regular intervals

- online activities for 3- to 10-year-olds

- counselling for young people and parents

- support through its Youth Agency for 11- to 20-year-olds with web pages to which they have exclusive access

- INSET

- publications.

The Association's website is at www.nagcbritain.org.uk.

Summary

- Schools must provide suitable challenge and appropriate support for their most able pupils.
- Appropriate provision can enhance motivation and improve behaviour.
- There are many agencies that can help teachers with this work.
- LEAs, as well as schools, have a duty to support the education of more able pupils.
- Ofsted teams expect to see suitable provision for the most able. It is an inclusion issue.
- School policy, with regard to more able children, must be reflected in practice.

CHAPTER 2

Departmental policy and approach

- Whole-school policy and its influence on departmental practice
- The roles and limitations of the gifted and talented school coordinator
- Developing music department policy for musically talented pupils
- Moving from policy to practice: practical implications from good policy documents
- Auditing provision and individual development planning for musically talented pupils

The development of a clear and distinct departmental policy for dealing with gifted and talented pupils is the responsibility of each head of department within the school. As we considered in Chapter 1, there is a requirement for all pupils to be given the opportunity to fulfil their potential within each curriculum area. Each department will need a clear policy statement to ensure that the teaching and learning programme that they are offering their pupils does, in practice, cater for all their pupils' varied needs as learners. This chapter will consider how whole-school policy will relate to departmental policy and practice. It will stress the need for all staff to work together to provide an educationally rich experience for gifted and talented pupils.

Importance of the whole-school context

Whatever the individual music department decides to write as policy and implement in practice has to be done in relationship to the general school policy that will be in place for gifted and talented pupils. It is important that the head of music has a clear understanding of the whole-school policy before seeking to apply it to the music department's own policy and working practices. Failure to do this will result in inadequate and disjointed provision for these pupils. Acknowledging the importance of the whole-school context will have a number of implications in several key areas of gifted and talented provision.

Identification and selection of gifted and talented pupils

Firstly, each school is expected to identify and select an gifted and talented (or 'able and talented') cohort of between 5 and 10 per cent in each academic year. Identification of gifted and talented pupils within a particular curriculum area can be fraught with difficulty. The construction of an appropriate process by which teachers can identify musically talented pupils is discussed at length in Chapter 3. For now, a brief definition drawn from the government's published literature will suffice as we consider the role of the music department in providing an appropriate educational environment for these pupils.

- 'Gifted' pupils are defined as having particular academic ability in one or more subjects in the statutory school curriculum other than art, music and PE.

- 'Talented' pupils will have aptitude in the arts or sports. (www.standards.dfes.gov.uk/giftedandtalented/guidanceandtraining/ roleofcoordinators/identificationofgt)

In the government's view, pupils cannot be gifted in art, music or PE but rather they should be designated as talented. The purpose and implication of such labelling will be discussed further in Chapter 3. But from now on, we shall be using the term 'musically talented' to describe this small group of pupils in each year group. This term was discussed and agreed on by a small group of eight heads of music formed to discuss key issues in this publication and drawn from schools around the North West of England.

The selection of musically talented pupils is fraught with conceptual and practical difficulties for the conscientious head of music. However, it is important that the head of music works in conjunction with other staff in the selection of these pupils. Given the prescription of 'talented' rather than 'gifted' in respect to musical ability, the music department policy will have to outline the practical steps that need to be taken to identify and support musically talented pupils both within the department and in conjunction with wider, whole-school provision and other enrichment opportunities.

Auditing arrangements and target-setting

Secondly, in order for departmental policy to work effectively alongside whole-school policy, the head of music will need to be aware of the individual auditing of pupils' prior knowledge and experience and the associated target-setting across the curriculum. This is particularly crucial as pupils cross between schools, e.g. at the end of Key Stage 2 into Key Stage 3.

Having identified a gifted and talented cohort for each academic year, schools are expected to undertake a thorough audit of those pupils' learning needs. These audits will result in individual attainment targets for each pupil that will challenge and stretch their abilities. They should also assist them in developing areas of relative weakness. These targets may focus on their acquisition of knowledge, thinking skills or learning process, but will also extend to cover such areas as motivation, participation, attendance and other issues related to pastoral support and development.

This auditing process, and the accompanying target-setting, will have consequences for each department. The head of music will have to be aware not only of which pupils have been identified on the gifted and talented register, but also what their particular individual targets are and how these can be best supported through their musical studies. It is important to remember that able or gifted pupils will have challenging targets that stretch them across the whole curriculum including music; musically talented pupils will have particular musical targets that will also need to be addressed. We will be considering some examples of good planning in Chapter 3. Specific target-setting for musically talented pupils will be considered in further detail below.

Different curriculum provision inside and outside the formal curriculum

There are a number of ways in which schools can meet the individual needs and associated targets for gifted and talented pupils. These will be discussed later in the book, where we will consider issues relating to the provision of opportunities within the classroom (Chapter 4), supporting learning (Chapter 5) and developing opportunities for extension and enrichment beyond the classroom (Chapter 6).

Here it is important to note that schools, and specifically the music department, will need to adopt a flexible approach to curriculum provision. It is possible, and in some cases likely, that musically talented pupils will be able to meet their individual targets and make appropriate progress solely through the standard, classroom-based provision provided to all pupils. However, in other situations there may well be the need for a range of other opportunities or different curricular arrangements in order for individual musically talented pupils to make good progress. This is not a matter of equality of access for all pupils, but rather it is about making sure that all pupils are given the opportunity to succeed.

Developing an appreciation of good practice

To help ensure that all pupils are given appropriate opportunities to succeed, the head of music will need to be aware of the wider opportunities available to pupils in the local area. This might include working alongside other school- or college-based music departments in local clusters, or working with other music professionals in alternative educational contexts such as community music groups, the local educational authority or private companies. Either way, music teachers should look both within and outside their immediate school context for sources of support for musically talented pupils. Working in isolation is not an option. As we all know, music teachers have all been far too busy for too long. It is time to start sharing the load.

Appropriate approaches to management

Music departments are busy places! There is a lot to do and often not enough time to do it in. Frequently, there is only one music teacher in the school, who has to act as head of music, chief technician, manager of peripatetic staff, concert promoter, exam coordinator and much more besides. The list of jobs often seems endless. One observer watching a music teacher work noted her fulfil the following tasks, all within a five-minute period of a music lesson:

- demonstrating using her own musical and technical skills

- being a musician composing and improvising on the hoof

- being a technician mending equipment

- listening to pupils playing their ideas

- moving pupils on faster by challenging them

- responding to pupils' requests, queries and interruptions

- suggesting refinements to pupils' work

- making sure of pupils' understanding by getting them to show what they meant rather than explain it

- making sure everyone got a turn on the equipment

- making observations and judgements about pupils' work

- correcting false information

- structuring pupils' practice

- giving pupils choices about how to proceed

- reminding pupils to save their work. (NAME 2000: 24)

Any music teacher would not be surprised at this list. But there is a danger of becoming so busy that it would be easy to brush over this vital role of ensuring that all musically talented pupils fulfil their potential.

Therefore, appropriate approaches to time and people management are vital. Part of this involves ensuring that good working relationships are established and maintained with the whole-school gifted and talented coordinator, whose role is outlined below. Additionally, busy heads of music can draw on each other's good working policies and practices to assist them in managing this important dimension of this work. It is hoped that the supplementary material contained on the accompanying CD will form a useful starting point for this work. But making use of the many free websites of teaching resources provided by other teachers, LEAs or university staff in education departments can also save valuable time. A list of some of these can be found in Appendix 2.1.

Ultimately, good time and people management can work alongside the construction of sensible and focused paper-based systems to ensure that those pupils identified on the gifted and talented registers do get the support that they need from the music department.

Centrality of the school gifted and talented coordinator

During the above discussion we have primarily considered the ways in which the overall work of the music department needs to be closely related to the school policies and practices in respect of gifted and talented pupils. We have examined this relationship through several themes that will recur throughout this book, namely the identification of musically talented pupils (Chapter 3), their support and the types of provision that individual departments should be offering them from work within the classroom (Chapter 4), the appropriateness of a range of wider academic and theoretical perspectives (Chapter 5) to extending and enriching opportunities outside the classroom when appropriate (Chapter 6).

Before we continue to look at the construction of an individual music department policy for musically talented pupils, it is essential to recognise the importance of one particular member of the school staff who is central to a head of music's work in this area, the school gifted and talented coordinator (G&T coordinator).

Role of the school G&T coordinator

A brief search of many government websites will reveal plenty of information about the role of the G&T coordinator (or the 'able and talented school coordinator' or ATSC). This discussion will focus primarily on some of the issues that pertain most closely to the work of the head of music.

Overall description

The G&T coordinator has a key leadership and management role to play in ensuring that all gifted and talented pupils receive an appropriately differentiated education that challenges and develops their skills and abilities. These coordinators have an overview of the gifted and talented cohorts in each year and are the head of music's first point of contact in any matters related to the provision of appropriate teaching and learning opportunities for such pupils. The G&T coordinator has a number of specific roles that the head of music can draw on.

Development, implementation, monitoring and evaluation of school policy

In forming their own departmental policies, heads of music will need to consider implementing key aspects of the school policy for their musically talented pupils. It would be advisable to build into departmental policy the same developmental, monitoring and evaluative strands of the school policy. The G&T coordinator will have such a developmental model in place for whole-school provision; working alongside this at departmental level will prevent problems, ensure commonality in approach and save valuable time.

Networking role

Part of the G&T coordinator's role will include working with coordinators from other schools, and building links with other providers. This is an invaluable opportunity for the head of music. As we have discussed already, there is an increasing need for music teachers to work in partnership with each other and to become more greatly aware of what is occurring in other schools or educational settings. Tapping into well-established networks will save time and energy. The networking that the G&T coordinator does could provide many benefits for the music department, including a greater awareness of pupils' musical aptitudes and abilities in previous key stages, opportunities for extension or enrichment activities within other institutional or educational contexts, as well as the possibility of making contact with, and bringing into the school, creative partners to work alongside pupils. There is also, of course, the opportunity for good practice to be shared between schools at a departmental level that could be initiated by the G&T coordinator. Finally, the G&T coordinator will also be a useful source of support in respect of national initiatives for gifted and talented pupils. The benefits of a number of these initiatives and collaborations will be explored in Chapter 6.

Collaborative work with departmental staff

The G&T coordinator is there to support the head of music in the preparation of a departmental policy and related practices. They will be able to advise on aspects relating to the identification of gifted and talented pupils and appropriate methods to audit their existing knowledge and skills, as well as set appropriately differentiated targets. Part of their role will be to ensure that the preparation, implementation and updating of good practice in this area is effectively linked to other school polices, e.g. on assessment, homework, home–school agreements and the maintenance of clear communication channels with parents.

Source of staff development

The G&T coordinator will be the initiator of any staff development activities that need to be undertaken in this area. There will be links here with continuing professional development opportunities for teachers and these may well be of interest to heads of music. At a more specific level, music teachers have a range of interesting problems with notions of giftedness and talent in music. As we will be discussing in the following chapters, the problems that these concepts present to us can become useful avenues of enquiry and exploration that may well result in the strengthening of music's place in the core curriculum. Sharing our concerns and issues about aspects of government policy in a constructive manner with the G&T coordinator can only lead to a more constructive and effectively differentiated curriculum for musically talented pupils.

Source of curriculum support

The G&T coordinator should be regarded as an expert on the needs of the gifted and talented cohort of pupils. As such, they should be consulted as the head of music seeks to design a curriculum that is appropriate to their needs. As we have already emphasised, the head of music will need to ensure that pupils who are designated as musically talented receive an appropriate curriculum experience as well as those designated as gifted in a general academic sense.

At a more mundane level, the G&T coordinator should have a good knowledge of current government policy in this area, e.g. the recent developments within the Key Stage 3 National Strategy's gifted and talented strand and other initiatives discussed in Chapter 1 will play a useful part in the head of music's policy formation and curriculum development.

Source of pupil support

Appropriately targeted support for individual pupils is central to effective teaching. Assessment for learning is central to this and is rightly a crucial plank in the Key Stage 3 National Strategy. The work done by music educators and researchers has played a very significant part in these developments. The G&T coordinator can give the head of music support and advice in devising appropriate assessment frameworks that lead to effective and appropriate support for gifted and talented pupils.

The linking role that the G&T coordinator plays in drawing together other school policies within the gifted and talented provision has a particular benefit here. All heads of department are expected to show how their individual departmental development plans are focused around and support whole-school priorities, e.g. the development of ICT as a teaching and learning resource, or approaches to creativity within the curriculum. The G&T coordinator will have a particular insight as to how these whole-school improvement issues will relate to specific music-department targets for the direct support of gifted and talented pupils.

Mentoring

The G&T coordinator is responsible for the organisation of any mentoring arrangements for gifted and talented pupils. The exact type of mentoring that is offered to these pupils will vary, but could include gifted and talented pupils:

- being mentored by older pupils

- acting as mentors for other pupils

- receiving mentoring from other teachers or support staff

- receiving mentoring from staff from other educational institutions or local businesses.

It will be important for the head of music to be aware of the type of mentoring activities that could be available for musically talented pupils in music. There may well be opportunities for local musicians, composers or other educators to work alongside the head of music in providing support for these pupils, perhaps in pursuing a common area of musical interest. The use of musical 'role models' or 'talent mentors' has been particularly beneficial for one school described in the case study that concludes Chapter 4. Similarly, the pupil peer-mentoring approach can have many positive musical benefits. Working on the principle that by teaching a musical skill or by helping develop musical understanding for someone else you are developing useful musical skills and understanding yourself, gifted and talented pupils can justifiably be used in a leadership role within the classroom. This is a notable feature of some of the pupil case studies presented in Chapter 3.

Extracurricular support/study support

Extracurricular activities are a feature of many music departments and, for the majority of heads of music, are crucial platforms on which musical talent and ability is nurtured and developed. They should provide opportunities for all pupils, and, in the best departmental practice, performance events are a natural and regular part of school life that give pupils a chance to share their performance and compositional skills in a way that builds confidence and leads towards independence.

The G&T coordinator can play a useful role in advising the head of music of extracurricular opportunities beyond the school boundaries. There are many opportunities for musically talented pupils in the local community and across the country. Part of the head of music's role will be to discuss these opportunities with the G&T coordinator and inform pupils and parents of the potentially enriching activities available to them outside of school hours.

Advocacy/champion

Finally, the G&T coordinator acts as 'the champion' of gifted and talented pupils within the school. They are responsible for the creation of a positive ethos and attitude towards such pupils. They should also ensure that the school policies and departmental practices reward and encourage the gifted and talented cohorts within each year group. This is a difficult and sensitive role. It would be easy to exclude such practices as elitist or exclusive, but reward systems in schools depend on effective classroom differentiation and the accurate understanding and appreciation of individual pupils' learning needs. All pupils deserve to be rewarded and praised when they achieve their learning objectives. The gifted and talented are no exception.

In summary, the G&T coordinator plays a crucial role in mediating between general school policies for the gifted and talented and the generation of specific departmental policy. They are the essential first stop for the head of music as they seek to write and implement departmental policy. They can offer the head of music the bigger picture of government provision for gifted and talented pupils and also act as a useful source of information, resources and opportunities for gifted and talented pupils in the local community or wider national context.

Limitations of the gifted and talented coordinator

As we have discussed above, the G&T coordinator will have a vital role in supporting the work of the head of music in this important area. However, it is essential that they are not seen as the sole authority on the identification of, and provision for, musically talented pupils. The G&T coordinator will have many strengths, but in relation to issues about specialist subject knowledge they will look to department heads for advice and leadership. It will be essential that the head of music has a firm understanding of what it means for a pupil to be musically talented, and how these pupils can be best identified and subsequently supported through a network of classroom-based and extracurricular provision both inside and outside the school. It is hoped that this book, drawn from the practices of many talented and inspirational heads of music, will prove a useful guide to others seeking to develop their work in this area.

Music department policy and practice

It is the responsibility of the head of music to form a departmental policy outlining the provision for musically talented pupils. This will be written in consultation with the G&T coordinator and will build upon the established themes of the whole-school policy for gifted and talented pupils. This important document will then form the basis of the department's practice in relation to musically talented pupils and should be monitored, evaluated and reviewed each year. In the following section we will consider the type of information that should be included within the department policy.

What to include in a musically talented department policy

The music department policy should follow the same framework as the school policy and fit in with its general philosophy. A good policy will develop from:

- a thorough and honest audit of existing levels of achievement of the most able and of their attitudes to learning
- clear identification of where changes need to be made and the drawing-up of an action plan
- consultation with senior management, G&T coordinator, other staff in the department and pupils
- the existence of effective strategies to monitor and evaluate the measures taken.

The following headings and questions could be used when preparing a music department policy for musically talented pupils:

Policy rationale and aims

- How does the departmental policy relate to the school's overall aims and values?

- How does musical study contribute to the young person's academic and personal development?

- What does the department aim to provide for musically talented students?

Definitions

- In the context of your school and department what do you mean by most able, able, gifted or talented in music?

Identification

- How does your department's approach to identifying these pupils fit in with the school's practice on identification?

- What subject-specific identification strategies will you use?

- Which types of data will you be collecting and analysing to make your decisions on who or who not to include on a list of gifted and talented pupils?

Organisational issues

- How will teaching groups be organised to meet the needs of all pupils including the musically talented?

- Will fast tracking, early entry or acceleration to an older age group be considered and what measures will be taken both to support these pupils and to ensure that they continue to make progress?

- What opportunities will the department provide for the mentoring of gifted and talented pupils?

Provision in lessons

- How do schemes of work and lesson plans reflect the demands to be made of musically talented pupils?

- How will the need for faster pace, more breadth and greater depth in musical knowledge and understanding be met?

- How will the thinking skills needed for music be developed?

- How will different learning styles of pupils be catered for?

- How will homework and independent learning be used to enhance pupils' musical learning?

- How will assessment, both assessment for learning and assessment of learning, be used to enable suitable targets to be set and appropriate progress to be made?

- How does the learning climate within the classroom support and encourage gifted and talented pupils?

Out-of-class activities

- How do opportunities for musically talented pupils beyond the classroom relate to the learning that takes place within the classroom?

- What specific systems of support for the most able are in place throughout the department's work?

- How is the department seeking to develop, nurture and sustain collaboration with outside agencies in the support of musically talented pupils?

Transfer and transition

- How is information from primary schools used to ensure progression throughout Key Stages 3 and 4?

- What measures are taken to assist musically talented pupils during their transition from primary to secondary school?

- How is the transition of musically talented pupils from the school's music department to other schools or colleges supported?

Resources

- How are teaching assistants, learning mentors and other adult helpers used to support musically talented pupils?

- What outside agencies are used to enforce this support when necessary or appropriate?

- What specific learning resources are available for musically talented pupils?

- How are information and communication technologies used to enhance the education of musically talented pupils?

Monitoring and evaluation

- Who is responsible for liaising with the G&T coordinator and developing good practice for the musically talented?

- How is the effectiveness of this policy to be measured?

- What targets does the department have for its gifted and talented students (e.g. Levels 7, 8 and exceptional at Key Stage 3, A or A* at GCSE)?

- How and when is the progress of individual pupils and groups monitored?

- Are there areas of continuing professional development that can be identified for staff within the department in order for the support of musically talented pupils to be improved?

These areas and questions are not exhaustive but should rather be used as a starting point for generating a good policy document. By way of illustration, a number of music department policy documents are included on the accompanying CD. Some of these follow the outline presented above, others differ significantly. As is always the case when writing these policy documents, the head of music will need to take into account the individual nature of their music department, its structure and working practices. It is fundamentally important, however, that the departmental policy be written in light of the general school policy on gifted and talented pupils.

In the course of planning for this publication, a number of schools were approached and asked to submit their written policy documents for musically talented pupils. One of these schools, West Leigh High School in Wigan, has written a particularly effective document that is worthy of further analysis.

Musically talented pupil policy (from West Leigh High School, developed in conjunction with Wigan LEA)

Identification of musically talented pupils

Pupils who are talented in music are likely to:

- be captivated by sound and engage fully with music

- select an instrument with care and then be unwilling to relinquish the instrument

- find it difficult not to respond physically to music

- memorise music quickly without any apparent effort, be able to repeat more complex rhythmical and melodic phrases given by the teacher and repeat melodies (sometimes after one hearing)

- sing and play music with a natural awareness of the musical phrase – the music makes sense

- demonstrate the ability to communicate through music, e.g. to sing with musical expression and with confidence

- show strong preferences, single-mindedness and a sustained inner drive to make music.

Pupils more often show their musical talent through the quality of their response than the complexity of their response. Musical quality is very difficult to define in words, as music is a different form of communication from language. The closest we can get is to say that it 'sounds right'; skills and techniques are used to communicate an intended mood or effect.

Therefore musical talent is at least as much about demonstrating a higher-quality response within levels as about attainment at higher levels. Musical talent can be seen at every level of attainment.

Pupils who have a talent for music show a particular affinity with sound. This type of talent is sometimes hard to identify, especially when it is not combined with more general giftedness. However, it is often most significant, since it may be a pupil's only route to real success, increasing their self-esteem and motivation for other areas of learning.

Some research points to the fact that there may be different types of intelligence, and that each of us may be more intelligent in some areas than others. This is often the case in music. Talented musicians may not demonstrate talent or giftedness in other areas.

Some teachers believe that music is only accessible for pupils with talent, that pupils are either musical, or not musical. This is not the case. All pupils can develop musical skills, knowledge and understanding. Some may need more or less help, but this is no different from any other subject. Teachers need to recognise the different needs of all pupils, including not only those who are talented but those who are more generally gifted across several subjects. The musically talented will need appropriate extension and development, while the more generally gifted pupils will need challenging musical contexts that enable them to apply their more general abilities.

Music provides a context in which generically gifted pupils (that is, those who are more generally gifted across several subjects) can be identified and developed. In music, pupils have to deal with a complex range of different and simultaneous factors and bring them together when making and responding to music. Teachers have often commented on the way that quickness in remembering rhythmic patterns suggests the ability to think quickly and assimilate information. Similarly, a difficulty with remembering patterns can indicate learning difficulties across all subjects. Teachers have found that music can help them to identify children who may need help.

Because music is abstract it provides a way of identifying and developing skills that are not language dependent. This means that it can play a particularly important part in helping to recognise giftedness in pupils whose language skills have not yet developed, especially those for whom English is not their first language.

Recognising talent in music

Musical talent may not be a constant potential that can be realised at any age. If the talent is to be fulfilled, it may have to be recognised at an early stage. This is especially true for some instrumental skills that require early development.

In secondary schools, there may be talented pupils who have not been recognised. These pupils need to be identified as early as possible, to ensure that their abilities are developed. In many cases, this will include providing opportunities for instrumental tuition for those who show musical talent.

Pupils who have already been having specialist lessons may present further challenges and will need to be encouraged to bring their instrumental skills into the classroom. Often the hardest challenge is to help these pupils balance their high levels of skill in performing on an instrument with the development of broader musical skills, knowledge and understanding, for example through creative activities.

Setting suitable learning challenges

Pupils who show musical talent will need to be given opportunities to extend their musical skills by learning an instrument and/or being helped to extend their vocal techniques and skills. They should use and extend these instrumental and vocal skills through performing, composing and appraising activities, both within and beyond the classroom. This will include performing with other talented pupils in school, regionally and, where appropriate, nationally.

Pupils who show more general giftedness will need to be mentally extended in music lessons. Teachers need to give them experiences that:

- challenge their ideas

- enable them to analyse and compare different pieces of music, including the use of musical scores and notations.

In addition, the pupils could use ICT to explore and use sounds expressively to a high level, without necessarily acquiring a comparative level of vocal or instrumental musical skill.

Selecting musical repertoire

Music heard in early childhood develops mental structures that affect how music is heard in later life. For example, if children hear mainly Western classical music when they are young, they become accustomed to the way that sounds are organised in this music and will be able to assimilate and use these structures easily in their own work. However, children whose experiences are from a different musical tradition will have a different set of codes and meanings, and will not be able to assimilate music from the Western tradition so easily.

Teachers need to be aware that the demonstration of giftedness or talent may be linked, in some part at least, to the type of music a pupil has experienced in early childhood. Young children need to be given opportunities to respond to a wide range of music before and during Key Stage 1. Those who are gifted and talented in music will then be able to discover a style, tradition or genre within which they can excel.

The issue of culture is particularly significant at Key Stage 3 where, because of adolescence, pupils are often less prepared to accept and appreciate music that is different. Teachers need to involve pupils through the careful use of music that will engage them and extend their understanding. This will demand a range of teaching strategies, as it is inevitable that a teacher's level of knowledge will vary considerably across a broad stylistic range.

Developing pupils who are gifted and talented

Musically talented pupils can be developed through:

- letting them take a lead

- setting them more challenging tasks and expecting a higher-quality response

- involving other skills that pupils have developed outside the classroom, e.g. instrumental skills

- providing open-ended tasks or new contexts in which to apply skills learned previously

- enabling pupils to improvise within given structures. Improvisation is an effective way to allow pupils to demonstrate and develop talent. As well as being extremely challenging, it enables pupils to respond at their own level

- extension work

- specialist tuition.

Specialist tuition can be essential, as it provides pupils with a voice with which to explore their own and others' ideas and feelings. It also provides real challenge that demands dedication, effort and self-discipline. This develops and extends all pupils – not just the talented.

In addition, teachers can develop pupils who are more generally gifted by:

- setting more demanding challenges in the classroom

- encouraging pupils to make more connection between ideas

- asking pupils to relate to music in the context in which it is created, performed and heard, to enable them to identify how music can be affected by different influences

- letting pupils set their own tasks and see them through

- allowing pupils to use a varying balance of practical work and research, so that they can choose to focus on discovering through listening and reading

- letting pupils help select areas for study and exploration

- asking pupils to analyse and evaluate music in relation to how it is constructed, produced and influenced

- giving them opportunities to practise and develop higher-level individual technical skills.

Talent in some aspects of music may not be a constant potential that can be realised at any age. In the case of some instrumental skills, for example, early development and training are highly desirable.

Analysis of West Leigh High School's policy

West Leigh High School's music department policy for musically talented pupils reminds us of some important foundational points that should be remembered by all music educators.

Musical talent can be developed

Firstly, the policy states clearly that musical talent is evidenced by the quality of pupils' responses rather than the complexity of their responses. In this chapter focusing on department policy and approach we need to remember that music is a subject that is inclusive rather than exclusive. It is something that all pupils can engage in, through which skills and understanding develop over time and as a result of good teaching. As West Leigh's policy document states, 'All pupils can develop musical skills, knowledge and understanding'. This will take place over time and the exact rate of development will differ from one pupil to another.

Musical talent is more than instrumental ability

Secondly, West Leigh's document reminds us that talent in music goes beyond instrumental ability. In fact, it points to a view that one of the hardest challenges for musically talented pupils may be in broadening their musical skills, knowledge and understanding through a range of creative activities that go beyond what could be a highly stylised or formal approach to musical performance. For example, the *Reflecting Others* project conducted at Debenham High School during 2001 found that those pupils with highly developed performance skills often found it the hardest to transfer to the world of digital audio mixing and processing, and associated compositional skills (Savage and Challis 2002). More information about this project can be found in Chapter 6.

Musical talent spreads beyond the classroom

Thirdly, we must remember that the music education offered to musically talented pupils does not exist in isolation from their wider musical experiences, both in other schools or colleges and within informal learning environments such as the playground, home or other community settings. As an example, we asked a female Year 10 musically talented pupil to keep a diary of her musical experiences during a typical week. The result makes fascinating reading and an extract can be found in Appendix 2.2. It serves as a useful reminder of how diverse our pupils' musical lives can be. There is no doubt that early life experiences in music may play a fundamental role in pupils' participation in musical activities as well as their notion of success or failure as musicians. Recent research into musical identity has shown the importance of these early experiences (MacDonald *et al.* 2002). Similarly, Lucy Green's work has revealed a huge range of alternative learning strategies that exist in the life stories of teenage and adult musicians that have developed outside the world of formal education (Green 2001).

Musical talent still means hard work and discipline

Finally, the West Leigh policy document reminds us that any kind of study requires dedication, effort and self-discipline. We could pursue a sporting metaphor here for a moment. Like music, physical education is another area within which the government believes pupils are talented rather than gifted. Perhaps they should consider the artistry of Roger Federer on the Centre Court at Wimbledon, or the pre-eminence of Tiger Woods' imperial display around St Andrews in the 2005 British Open. No serious commentators would argue against the case for each of these sportsmen exhibiting something close to giftedness in their chosen sport. But the point here is that these gifted sportsmen have, in an almost equal measure, dedicated their lives to hard work, effort and discipline in pursuit of excellence.

Music teachers have responsibilities to supporting the musically talented through a range of strategies. But all talent needs to be backed up by hard work and self-discipline. All pupils need to be reminded of this on occasions, however talented or gifted they may appear to be.

From policy to practice

Having written the policy document, the head of music will want to use it to ensure the department's good practice. Implementing the policy is a vital strand in ensuring that musically talented pupils experience the benefit of the music department's sound thinking in this area.

A vital first phase in this transition from policy to practice is the auditing of provision for musically talented pupils. Kingsdown High School in Wigan supplied an interesting example that audited their provision for the academic year 2003/4 (as shown in the table opposite).

Their audit highlights the division between curriculum extension and enrichment activities. These are common distinctions in the literature relating to the support of gifted and talented pupils. Curriculum extension relates to the opportunities available to pupils within the classroom through extending activities in particular ways; enrichment relates to opportunities available to these pupils outside the context of the music lesson, either within or outside the school.

This kind of simple plan is a useful summary of provision across each year group that mediates between the grand policy statement and day-to-day practice. A generic checklist that may be useful to heads of music has been provided on the accompanying CD. However, it is also vital that heads of music consider the specific needs of individual pupils. This is where the practice of writing individual education plans (IEPs) is potentially so useful.

Alongside the audit of overall provision for musically talented pupils at Key Stage 3, Kingsdown High School has also supplied two examples of IEPs: Darren Walker (Year 9) and Vicky Booth (Year 7).

Audit of talented provision in music 2003/4

Year group	Pupil activity	Opportunity for curriculum extension	Enrichment	Date introduced	Participation of G&T cohort involved	Effectiveness
Year 7	1. Enhancing natural rhythm	• Complex rhythm patterns in composition	• Dance club	September 2003	75%	Opening up students' minds and imaginations to different musical cultures and musical experiences. Enjoyment of 'dance'.
	2. Use of the voice	• Class singing in harmony	• Choir • Visits to different schools, e.g. Hope School; the Road Show visits	January 2003	75%	Positive effect on peers, 'choir is cool'. There are now 50 members.
Year 8	Instrumental lessons	• Use of instruments in 'class band' • Use of instruments to demonstrate techniques • Use in composition to create different textures • Performance practice	• Choir • Samba Band • Instrumental lessons with professional tutors • Workshops	September 2003	100%	Boost in confidence. Positive effect on the year group in music. Student progression increased. Enjoyment and positive feedback
Year 9	1. Instrumental lessons 2. Performance practice	• Use of instruments in 'class band' • Demonstration of techniques and for use in listening tasks • Use in composition and performances • Set time aside within the curriculum to work on a set piece or composition with the same theme as is being taught to the rest of the class	• Choir • Samba band • Ensemble work • Instrumental lessons • Workshops	September 2003	100%	Music is 'cool', very positive effect on the underachieving students in Year 9. They are encouraged by the change in the 'ethos' of music at the school. Students benefit from individual tuition and they appreciate time spent on them.

From Kingsdown High School in conjunction with Wigan LEA

Individual education plan: Darren Walker

The gifted or talented musician will show some of the following characteristics:

✓ An innate sense of rhythm

✓ An ability to use an instrument well

   An appreciation of other musicians

   Dedication

   A longer than average concentration span

   An ability to attempt to play well-known tunes instinctively

   Good dexterity

They may be extended by:

- Extending their composition skills with reference to harmony, etc.
- Learning to play in the style of . . .
- Evaluating their own and others' performances both live and through recordings

Comments

Darren is a Year 9 student.
He is talented at playing the drums.
He has instrumental tuition.
He has good musical knowledge and understanding in general.
He gets extremely frustrated if he cannot grasp a musical concept straightaway. I am working on different strategies to introduce more complex musical idioms in his learning without causing angst and confusion.

Individual education plan				
Number: 1	**Date:** September 2003	**Student:** Darren Walker	**Group:** 9	**Tutor:**
What (targets and standards to be reached)		**How** (methods, activities and resources)		**Who/Where/When** (frequency, input by, duration, location)
<ul><li>To be more positive about his own talent and ability</li><li>To use the facilities in school to improve his drumming skills</li><li>To develop skills via working with other drummers in an ensemble situation</li><li>A calm rational approach needs to be adopted to ensure that Darren reaches his potential</li></ul>		<ul><li>Drumming lessons</li><li>Check notice board and book the drum studio for rehearsals</li><li>Work with the other drummers in school. Look at different skills and experiment with different drumming patterns and rhythms</li><li>Careful explanation of theoretical matters with practical examples</li><li>Build in 'one to one' teaching</li></ul>		<ul><li>The drum tuition is once a week for half an hour</li><li>Studio is open every day after school and lunchtime slots are available</li><li>Ensemble situations will be set up on a regular basis</li><li>Handouts and extra material are available to aid understanding and musical progression</li></ul>

Sample IEP: Darren Walker (developed by Kingsdown High School in conjunction with Wigan LEA)

Individual education plan: Vicky Booth

The gifted or talented musician will show some of the following characteristics:

✓ An innate sense of rhythm

 An ability to use an instrument well

✓ An appreciation of other musicians

 Dedication

 A longer than average concentration span

✓ An ability to attempt to play well-known tunes instinctively

 Good dexterity

They may be extended by:

● Extending their composition skills with reference to harmony, etc.

● Learning to play in the style of . . .

● Evaluating their own and others' performances both live and through recordings

Comments

Vicky is a Year 7 student.
She has demonstrated the above and is very enthusiastic.
She picks 'musical' material, both practical and theoretical, up well.
She participates in the curriculum enrichment and extracurricular activities.
Vicky will be monitored closely and she needs to be encouraged to progress at every level.

Individual education plan				
Number: 1	**Date:** September 2003	**Student:** Vicky Booth	**Group:** 7	**Tutor:**
What (targets and standards to be reached)		**How** (methods, activities and resources)	**Who/Where/When** (frequency, input by, duration, location)	
● Clear focus at the start of the lesson to avoid 'giddiness' and loss of concentration ● Use of planner: organisational techniques to help her remember when the extracurricular activities are taking place ● Evaluating her own progress and achievement ● Increase in her motivation around peers		● Style Fusion ● Dance Club ● Participation in the 'choir' weekend away with the National Youth Choir coach ● Instrumental tuition ● Ensemble work	● Reminders regularly from music teacher ● Encouragement in class ● Use of her talents to illustrate teaching points ● 'Thinking skills' to develop her learning skills in general ● Style Fusion and Dance Club for 45 minutes after school each week. Extra choir session on Thursday lunchtimes.	

Sample IEP: Vicky Booth (developed by Kingsdown High School in conjunction with Wigan LEA)

Both IEPs follow the same format. The opening section lists a number of potential characteristics that musically talented pupils might exhibit. This is a useful reminder for teachers as to what constitutes musical talent. It is something that will be considered in more detail in Chapter 3 when we look at the precise factors that identify a musically talented pupil.

The second main section allows for the teacher to list some general remarks about the pupil. These may relate to musical abilities or skills, but often focus on other factors that may affect the pupil's learning. Darren, for example, has a propensity towards frustration when he fails to grasp a new concept quickly; Vicky is very enthusiastic but prone to a loss of concentration that can lead to her becoming demotivated. Other staff may have picked up these more general points. Perhaps the G&T coordinator has shared them with heads of department. Either way, they are useful points to bear in mind as the IEP moves into its final stage.

The final stage of the IEP gets down to the nitty-gritty of what these pupils are going to try to achieve during the current academic year. It needs to be the product of negotiations between the pupil and the head of music. It may involve the work of other adults, including other departmental staff, and peripatetic or private tutors, who will need to be informed of its content. The model of IEP that Kingsdown High School has adopted seems particularly useful. It is focused around a set of three questions:

- What?

- How?

- Who, where and when?

Once again, we can notice a focus on musical skills, understanding and knowledge working alongside other educational interventions to ensure that these pupils make the most of their abilities. Darren is being urged to develop a more positive attitude towards his drumming, particularly in working alongside other drummers within the school whom he should look towards for help in developing different skills, patterns and rhythms. Alongside this, he needs to develop a calmer and more rational approach to learning new concepts. This has a direct implication for the teacher, who is going to match new theoretical content with practical examples within a one-to-one teaching context where possible.

What we can also note from Darren's IEP are the whole-school implications. Darren's work within the classroom and the strategies that the teacher is going to adopt are going to change; his social relationship to other musicians and the development of his ensemble playing skills will progress; his organisational skills in turning up for drum lessons and booking practice facilities have been highlighted; finally, his psychological perspective of his ability and how he is going to develop this further without causing 'angst and confusion' is a key target.

Similarly, if we study Vicky's IEP we can trace common elements relating to teaching and learning, social, organisational and psychological factors. Here, and through negotiation with the teacher, the plan has identified particular periods in music lessons where concentration is demanded and expected. The teacher's role is clearly detailed. Reminders and gentle encouragement at the beginning of lessons will be accompanied by Vicky's active involvement in demonstrating teaching points throughout the lesson. Socially, the plan is seeking to promote Vicky's engagement in music-making more widely than the classroom context (which appears to be where it has been limited to so far). So Vicky is attending Style Fusion and Dance Club after school each week and participating in a weekend away with a National Youth Choir coach. Organisationally, Vicky is urged to make better use of her planner to keep track of her greater number of commitments. Finally, at a psychological level Vicky's targets relate to her evaluating her own progress and achievements more formally as well as her making a conscious effort to show a greater sense of motivation in her musical work when working alongside her peers. It appears that Vicky needs careful monitoring and is prone to take the easy pathway if it is offered to her. Ensuring that Vicky makes the most of her musical talent will not be easy. But it is clear to see within this IEP that the teacher and Vicky have come together to agree a common framework for her educational development that addresses her needs across a range of areas that move beyond purely musical concerns.

Summary

- Departmental policy relating to musically talented pupils must be written in light of whole-school policy for gifted and talented pupils.
- Heads of music must work in close collaboration with the G&T coordinator.
- Departmental policy must be clearly worked out in practice.
- Auditing provision is a vital first step in the department rationalising its approach towards musically talented pupils.
- Individual education plans personalise department policy and focus teachers' and musically talented pupils' efforts throughout the year.

CHAPTER 3

Recognising high ability and potential

- Identification of musically talented pupils is a complicated process
- There are various definitions and indicators of musical talent
- Musically talented pupils will display a range of characteristics that can be spotted by the discerning teacher
- Case studies of musically talented pupils help to share perspectives and approaches to identification of, and provision for, musically talented pupils
- Identification of musically talented pupils will require the head of music to work through a clear process
- Baseline assessment is an important tool in identifying musically talented pupils and sharing judgements across local schools

Openings . . .

Alex's music is a revelation to me. Dark, moody, highly expressive and emotionally charged, it has that indefinable quality that ensures it stands out and makes you listen. It is entrancing and alluring. It beckons you into new sonic landscapes where imagination and emotion can run free. Being invited into Alex's world is always an education. I look forward to my visits to his studio, to hear about his current projects and to listen to his latest musical ideas. Some examples of his music can be found on the accompanying CD.

I met Alex for the first time in 2002. I visited him as part of a songwriting research project at his home in a deprived part of South Manchester near Old Trafford, the Manchester United football ground. On arriving, I remembered the words of Stuart Hall, long time radio football commentator – the 'Theatre of Dreams' I think he once called it. Strong coffee in hand, Alex leads me down the narrow basement stairs to a large space, partitioned into three areas by bookcases and pieces of equipment.

One space is devoted to recordings, thousands upon thousands of CDs from music styles drawn from far and wide. Here Bach rubs shoulders with Cage, Rachmaninov with Eminem, obscure African songs with German lieder and everything in-between. I feel humbled by the breadth of his knowledge about his massive collection. He draws out CD after CD. 'Have you heard of this?' he asks, 'Or this?' All too often the answer is no. Many of the artists and composers' names are unfamiliar and their music distant from my own listening. But I recognise the complete set of Sibelius symphonies.

The second space is full of books (and more CDs). Many are philosophical – discussing aspects of musical composition and technology, the kind you would expect to see in a university library. There is contemporary fiction here too, and books on other art forms such as film, video art and photography.

The final space is the heart of Alex's creative existence, his theatre of dreams. Cosseted under a small basement skylight, a dark and atmospheric space with a range of ambient lighting, here is the recording studio where his dreams become reality. There is just space for the two of us, and his dog, to settle down. Computers, synthesisers, samplers, a large mixing desk and other pieces of technology old and new surround us. Many of these pieces of equipment are fairly common in other studios. But I am about to find out that there is nothing common about Alex's music or the story of how he began to create it.

We start to talk. I suggest we go back to the beginning. I presume that his music education started early? What did he remember about music in his primary school?

I played the xylophone – briefly. I remember the headmaster having me in the school assembly playing 'God Save the Queen'. After that I just fazed out – I was nine years old. I didn't like the attention from people and I found it too much – the attention of all those faces watching me play that. Since then I've always been very opposed to performing in front of people. I rarely do gigs.

Not the most positive of starts I thought. I move quickly on to high school. Who was his high-school music teacher? What did he remember about him or her?

[11 seconds silence] I'm struggling . . . I remember my history teacher very well. I had burning interest in history so I remember him very well. [5 seconds silence] Music – I mean – what they taught you was Baroque and Bach, Mozart and Beethoven and completely lost on kids. It's such a refined poetry that, you know, these composers who now I spend a lot of money collecting their stuff, is lost on kids.

In fact, the whole school experience was not a positive one:

I was excluded from school when I was 15 years old. I'm 29 now and have hindsight on my side. I see points that were causing the trouble. But I also think that there were some elements at school that perhaps did 'fail' me. I think that one of the more important things that the teachers could have done was recognise my passionate nature and harness that, to bring out the best in me rather than put it to one side and be lazy and just exclude me.

I am intrigued to know what he makes of his own work. How does he define his unique studio practice? What does he think musical composition is about? What is his definition of a musician?

> There are hundreds of examples. But from someone who has never been taught where the C note is, for me composition starts with John Cage's Silence and ends with Rachmaninov. And in-between there's a small child who presses down a couple of notes on the keyboard or piano. They're a musician. . . . Of course their language is underdeveloped but they have that potential to go from that Cagian silence to Rachmaninov through practice and learning. There's no real defined point – you are a musician.

As our conversation draws to an end, Alex speaks in quasi-religious terms about the 'saving power' of music in his life.

> Music is – how can I describe it, it's so many things – it really has saved me from a life that – it's hard to explain. I grew up on an estate in Edinburgh and I used to get in quite a lot of trouble. Music saved me from a path that I could see leading to destruction and for that I'm very grateful. So I tend to treat music as a very good friend. It's something that's helped me to communicate with people, to express myself. It's a language that you can relate to people from different nations. It transcends limitations.

Alex's story encapsulates one of the current problems that formal music education has to face. He is unable to play a musical instrument in any traditional sense, is entirely self-taught as a composer but successful commercially (writing music for television, film and other digital media), highly articulate in his views of others' music and consumed by a commitment and passion for his own. Yet here is a talented and gifted composer for whom the world of formal music education at best was a total irrelevance (and at worst it failed him completely).

As we discussed in Chapter 2, there is no single and simple definition for what a musically talented pupil in music looks like. Given this obvious statement, it is clear that identifying talent in music presents a significant challenge for the music teacher. What this chapter will seek to do is present a series of options for music teachers seeking to develop their practice of identifying musically talented pupils. It will consider a range of evidence in respect of definitions, characteristics and descriptions before moving on to illustrate a number of musically talented pupils through case studies written by their teachers. Finally, it will present a practical strategy that teachers can adopt and implement to assist this part of their ongoing work.

Defining ability

Defining what ability or talent means is a very difficult task for any teacher. Within music education the issue is particularly acute. Precise definitions of what it is to be 'musical' are very hard to pin down. Within the context of schools and classrooms, it is not just about spotting pupils who are good at something already. It is about spotting potential and then nurturing and supporting this through appropriate educational intervention.

The process by which we might define musical talent is shaped by at least two important themes.

Anecdotal evidence of ability

Firstly, as teachers we can all generate anecdotal evidence to support what we believe are the characteristics of a particular musically talented pupil. These might be built on our beliefs or experience of what is valued within our musical culture. These ideas about talent or ability are socially and culturally constructed and subject to change over time. It is unlikely that we would share the same view as a Victorian music educator in respect of the skills or understandings a musically talented pupil might exhibit. Similarly, the musical skills and understandings in young people generated in an alternative cultural setting would be very different. But we should recognise that at a general level what teachers think and believe about their pupils has an effect on what they might learn.

Scientific indicators of ability

Secondly, within the world of social science there are important and significant debates about how to define ability, particularly in the role of IQ and creativity as indicators of ability in certain subject areas. These are neatly, and probably problematically, summarised within the 'nature' or 'nurture' debate that is regularly rehearsed amongst educators.

Another problematic simplification is the quantitative or qualitative divide. Those with a quantitative disposition might argue that raw talent can be numerically defined within a cohort of pupils and discovered by an appropriate range of statistical tests; those with a qualitative streak might be considering ability as being uncovered as pupils are given access to appropriate educational resources and opportunities. Either way, the philosophical and psychological arguments here are highly sophisticated and well beyond the scope of this chapter.

What remains beyond doubt is that the government has given a clear definition for gifted and talented pupils. As we will come to see, this definition may well be considered a problem for many music educators.

There are many definitions of gifted and talented. This guidance builds on the work of Excellence in Cities (EiC), which identifies:

- 'gifted' learners as those who have abilities in one or more subjects in the statutory school curriculum other than art and design, music and PE.

- 'talented' learners as those who have abilities in art and design, music, PE, or performing arts such as dance and drama.

This guidance uses the phrase 'gifted and talented' to describe all learners with gifts and talents.

EiC targets gifted and talented work at the top 5–10% of pupils in any school, regardless of the overall ability profile of pupils. Many schools and local education authorities outside EiC have adopted similar criteria, while others use alternative benchmarks.

While the EiC definition relates to the national curriculum and to pupils of compulsory school age, it may be extended to include those who show marked abilities in any area of the school or college curriculum at any age. It is not unusual for older students to show significant ability and enthusiasm when they take up new areas of the curriculum and have a new context for study (www.nc. uk.net/gt/general/index.htm).

This broad definition frames the work of teachers in school. It does not allow for a pupil to be gifted in music. Rather, they are to be described as talented. It sets a limit on the number of pupils falling within the categories of 'gifted' or 'talented' at between 5% and 10% of an overall year group of pupils. These distinctions are obviously artificial and arbitrary. They could be easily disputed and challenged on a range of educational and psychological research evidence. This is why, for the purposes of this book, a group of teachers have defined these pupils as being 'musically talented'. By this, we mean pupils who are obviously excelling in music activity, whether that is practical or theoretical in nature. We also use this term to encompass any pupils who might be perceived to have a musical 'gift' of some sort.

General characteristics of the gifted and talented pupil

There has been a lot of research that has sought to identify the general characteristics of the gifted and talented pupil. It is important for all teachers to be aware of these issues in a general sense as they will implicate the more specific subject-based characteristics that we will discuss below. Jane Petrie has developed the following list in conjunction with Wigan LEA.

Speech

Gifted or talented students may:

- speak in a manner normally associated with an adult
- use superior vocabulary than their peers – they may use more complex sentences, possibly with more than one subordinate clause
- use grammar accurately
- prefer to speak their ideas, rather than write them down, as some feel that the physical act of writing slows down their thought processes
- be very good readers, and may have shown an interest in reading, even at a pre-school age.

Learning

Gifted or talented students may:

- show a great interest in a wide variety of things, and express a willingness to learn

- be capable of understanding quite complicated information

- possess a very probing questioning technique

- choose to skip some stages in the learning process

- not warm to authority

- develop good observational skills.

Thinking

Gifted or talented students may:

- have good reasoning skills

- be able to take concrete ideas and formulate an abstract

- overlook obvious relationships in favour of the unusual

- show great perception

- develop ideas in a lateral fashion

- enjoy working with abstractions, e.g. programming computers, inventing pastimes

- be very interested in news or current affairs

- have unusual interests, e.g. fantasy role-play

- appear almost fanatical in their interest for a hobby.

Motivation

Gifted or talented students may:

- have the ability to extend a task

- be able to stay on-task for long periods of time when absorbed

- be very critical of their own output.

Relationships

Gifted or talented students may:

- challenge arguments and possibly appear to be disrespectful
- prefer the company of adults
- take an interest in difficult discussion areas such as politics or religious debate
- be the dominant one in their social group.

Humour

Gifted or talented students:

- often have a quirky sense of humour favouring the absurd
- may use subtle humour to great effect.

Technical

Gifted or talented students may show understanding of complex technical items such as car engines or electronics.

Morality

Gifted or talented students:

- will probably have strong ideas about what is right and wrong
- may have unnecessary worries.

Characteristics of underachievers

Similarly, pupils that are underachieving but who may be gifted or talented exhibit a number of characteristics that teachers will be able to spot. Being able to identify these general features and work through them with pupils is another important step in identifying potentially gifted or talented pupils.

Underachievers often demonstrate behaviour that can be anti-social, and fail to attain their true ability. They may:

- be against school and, in particular, against authority
- be articulate, but poor at expressing ideas on paper
- be dismissive of praise
- be bored
- have poor emotional control

- be introverted

- be rude to and about other students

- be lacking in competitiveness

- be very self-critical

- be dismissive of their own abilities

- be unable to mix socially, or they may mix exclusively with other poor achievers

- be apparently in control of the situation

- be split personalities in and out-of-school.

But they may:

- show strong ability in areas in which they are interested

- learn quickly

- be good problem solvers

- show abstract thought

- ask 'awkward' but incisive questions

- persevere strongly in areas that motivate them.

They are hard to identify and they go unnoticed because:

- they deceive very easily because they are well practised; they have tactics to avoid discovery

- it is often difficult to differentiate between underachievers and those with poor abilities; few, if any, tests will reveal them

- teachers are over-stretched, and do not have the time to identify them

- our views of what makes a gifted or talented student vary

- we know little about how to motivate them and allow their skills to develop

- many parents are unsupportive.

Subject-specific characteristics of musically talented pupils

More generally, what should music teachers be attempting to identify in selecting musically talented pupils? There are a number of guides or systems that could be adapted to assist teachers in their identification of musically talented children. We will consider two such frameworks here.

National Curriculum levels of attainment by curriculum area

Level	Attainment targets			
	Overarching statement	Performing skills	Composing skills	Listening/appraising skills
1	Pupils recognise and explore how sounds can be made and changed.	They use their voices in different ways such as speaking, singing and chanting, and perform with awareness of others.	They repeat short rhythmic and melodic patterns and create and choose sounds in response to given starting points.	They respond to different moods in music and recognise well-defined changes in sounds, identify simple repeated patterns and take account of musical instructions.
2 (Expected attainment at the end of Key Stage 1)	Pupils recognise and explore how sounds can be organised.	They sing with a sense of the shape of the melody, and perform simple patterns and accompaniments to a steady pulse.	They choose carefully and order sounds within simple structures such as beginning, middle, end, and in response to given starting points.	They represent sounds with symbols and recognise how the musical elements can be used to create different moods and effects. They improve their own work.
3	Pupils recognise and explore the ways sounds can be combined and used expressively.	They sing in tune with expression and perform rhythmically simple parts that use a limited range of notes.	They improvise repeated patterns and combine several layers of sound with awareness of the combined effect.	They recognise how the different musical elements are combined and used expressively and make improvements to their own work, commenting on the intended effect.
4 (Expected attainment at the end of Key Stage 2)	Pupils identify and explore the relationship between sounds and how music reflects different intentions.	While performing by ear and from simple notations they maintain their own part with awareness of how the different parts fit together and the need to achieve an overall effect.	They improvise melodic and rhythmic phrases as part of a group performance and compose by developing ideas within musical structures.	They describe, compare and evaluate different kinds of music using an appropriate musical vocabulary. They suggest improvements to their own and others' work, commenting on how intentions have been achieved.
5 (Expected attainment at the end of Key Stage 3; or below)	Pupils identify and explore musical devices and how music reflects time and place.	They perform significant parts from memory and from notations with awareness of their own contribution such as leading others, taking a solo part and/or providing rhythmic support.	They improvise melodic and rhythmic material within given structures, use a variety of notations and compose music for different occasions using appropriate musical devices such as melody, rhythms, chords and structures.	They analyse and compare musical features. They evaluate how venue, occasion and purpose affect the way music is created, performed and heard. They refine and improve their work.

Level				
6 (Expected attainment at the end of Key Stage 3; or above)	Pupils identify and explore the different processes and contexts of selected musical genres and styles.	They select and make expressive use of tempo, dynamics, phrasing and timbre. They make subtle adjustments to fit their own part within a group performance.	They improvise and compose in different genres and styles, using harmonic and non-harmonic devices where relevant, sustaining and developing musical ideas and achieving different intended effects.	They use relevant notations to plan, revise and refine material. They analyse, compare and evaluate how music reflects the contexts in which it is created, performed and heard. They make improvements to their own and others' work in the light of the chosen style.
7	Pupils discriminate and explore musical conventions in, and influences on, selected genres, styles and traditions.	They perform in different styles, making significant contributions to the ensemble and using relevant notations.	They create coherent compositions drawing on internalised sounds and adapt, improvise, develop, extend and discard musical ideas within given and chosen musical structures, genres, styles and traditions.	They evaluate, and make critical judgements about the use of musical conventions and other characteristics and how different contexts are reflected in their own and others' work.
8	Pupils discriminate and exploit the characteristics and expressive potential of selected musical resources, genres, styles and traditions.	They perform, improvise and compose extended compositions with a sense of direction and shape, both within melodic and rhythmic phrases and overall form.	They explore different styles, genres and traditions, working by ear and by making accurate use of appropriate notations and both following and challenging conventions.	They discriminate between musical styles, genres and traditions, commenting on the relationship between the music and its cultural context, making and justifying their own judgements.
Exceptional performance	Pupils discriminate and develop different interpretations.	They express their own ideas and feelings in a developing personal style exploiting instrumental and/or vocal possibilities. They give convincing performances and demonstrate empathy with other performers.	They produce compositions that demonstrate a coherent development of musical ideas, consistency of style and a degree of individuality.	They discriminate and comment on how and why changes occur within selected traditions including the particular contribution of significant performers and composers.

© QCA 2001 (adapted from www.ncaction.org.uk/subjects/music/levels.htm)

National Curriculum levels of attainment

The most well-known framework that teachers have to work with for the assessment of pupils' skill, knowledge and understanding is the National Curriculum levels of attainment (www.ncaction.org.uk/subjects/music/levels.htm). The benefit of this system is that it is something which teachers are used to working with, they are familiar with its content and, despite initial difficulties, they will have learnt to use it constructively within their teaching. But teachers will need to consider what practical skills pupils will acquire through this model of music development. The level descriptors for the attainment target contain some interesting statements, some of which are only dubiously developmental, if at all (DfEE 1999: 36–77). Each statement opens with a general statement of attainment and is followed by a description of that statement in respect of performing, composing and listening outcomes. The table on the previous pages lists these statements in respect of the performing, composing and listening/appraising component for each level.

There are two important features of the attainment target and levels that should be carefully noted. Firstly, just like the knowledge, skills and understanding strands of each key stage, there is a sense of accumulation in the level strands of the attainment target. 'Discriminating and exploring musical conventions in selected genres, styles and traditions' (Level 7) does not replace the need to 'recognise and explore the ways sounds can be combined and used expressively' (Level 3). Both aspects should be evidenced in a pupil's work at Level 7. Similarly 'singing in tune and with expression' (Level 3) is not replaced by 'performing in different styles, making significant contributions to the ensemble and using relevant notations' (Level 7) otherwise the results would be ridiculous.

Secondly, in relation to the practical use of the attainment target and levels the National Curriculum document is very clear: 'The level descriptions provide the basis for making judgements about pupils' performance *at the end of Key Stages 1, 2 and 3*' [my emphasis] (DfEE 1999: 36). The legal requirement is for teachers to make use of these level statements in a final report, perhaps to parents, at the end of the key stage. Whatever the assessment coordinators within schools say, for music they were not designed to be a week-by-week assessment device or a means of assessing pupil achievement at the end of a scheme of work. There might be a case for teachers legitimately using the content of the level statements to assist their process of regular assessment and help define appropriate learning objectives in their planning. But the overuse of such a mechanistic approach would be detrimental to a pupil's overall musical development. Similarly, using solely these criteria as a means to identify pupils who were musically talented would be a catastrophic error.

Bloom's taxonomy of learning

Perhaps more helpfully, Bloom's taxonomy (Bloom 1956) was originally created as a framework for categorising levels of questioning. In Chapter 4 we will consider it in this way as a useful assessment for learning tool. Here we can see

Bloom's overview of learning through a number of stages, working up from knowledge and finishing in evaluation:

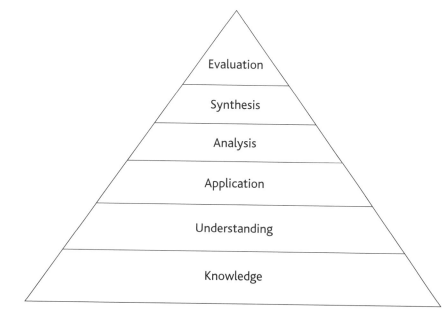

Bloom's taxonomy

Through examining Bloom's descriptions of questioning types or categories we can begin to see the characteristics of each 'level' of learning. The table on pages 48 and 49 illustrates these characteristics and gives them a musical context through suggested examples related to a pupil's ability as a performer, composer and listener/appraiser of music.

Case studies of musically talented pupils

These two frameworks give some useful ideas as to the types of musical skills or abilities pupils might exhibit. They attempt to level these in various ways but, of course, this can lead to philosophical problems or musical differences of opinion. One only has to consider the types of knowledge that are 'officially' valued by examination boards at GCSE or A level to see that no national system is going to meet with everyone's approval.

There are alternative methods by which teachers can begin to share understandings as to what would constitute a musically talented pupil. But perhaps the most useful way of seeking to develop a strategy for the identification of musically talented pupils is to examine the work of other teachers in this area, to share ideas and views as to what they have identified as being worthy of exceptional music talent and how they have sought to nurture it once discovered. The opportunity to have these discussions between and across schools is often difficult. Just getting on with the job of teaching oneself is demanding enough and opportunities for teachers to obtain 'time out' to share ideas and good practice with other teachers are limited. Within this book we have been very grateful for the contributions of several teachers who have been grappling with these issues

Bloom's taxonomy applied to musical learning

Learning type	Definition	Keywords	Key skills	Possible musical applications
Knowledge	Exhibits previously learnt material by recalling facts, terms, basic concepts and answers	Who, what, why, when, omit, where, which, choose, find, how, define, label, show, spell, list, match, name, relate, tell, recall, select	• Observation and recall of information • Knowledge of dates, events and places • Mastery of subject matter • Knowledge of major ideas	Pupils can: • accurately perform pieces • compose following a series of instructions • recall and show musical concepts related to music theory, history and style
Understanding	Demonstrates an understanding of facts and ideas by organising, comparing, translating, interpreting, giving descriptions and stating main ideas	Compare, contrast, demonstrate, interpret, explain, extend, illustrate, infer, outline, relate, rephrase, translate, summarise, show, classify	• Understanding of information • Grasp of meaning • Translation of knowledge into new context • Interpretation of facts, comparison, contrast • Ordering, grouping, inferring causes • Predicting consequences	Pupils can: • accurately perform pieces demonstrating or illustrating a range of possible musical interpretations • compose beyond given instructions, outlining and inferring possible compositional opportunities within the given style • grasp musical meanings within listening activities and translate these meanings across a range of contexts
Application	Solving problems by applying acquired knowledge, facts, techniques and rules in a different way	Apply, build, choose, construct, develop, interview, make use of, organise, experiment with, plan, select, solve, utilise, model, identify	• Using information • Using methods, concepts, theories in new situations • Solving problems using required skills or knowledge	Pupils can: • draw lessons from various difference performance opportunities and apply these constructively within a new performance context • show an extensive flair for freely experimenting with and developing musical ideas within a composition project and to organise these into a coherent whole, justifying their choices throughout • respond to music in an imaginative way, applying musical knowledge and understanding in unusual ways

Analysis	Examining and breaking information into parts by identifying motives or causes; making inferences and finding evidence to support generalisations	Analyse, categorise, classify, compare, contrast, discover, dissect, divide, examine, inspect, simplify, survey, take part in, test for, distinguish, list, distinction, theme, relationships, function, motive, inference, assumption, conclusion	• Seeing patterns • Organisation of parts • Recognition of hidden meanings • Identification of components	Pupils can: • understand, appreciate and seek to convey their own musical interpretation of a given performance piece • show a clearly analytical approach to musical composition and develop an understanding of how musical ideas are generated, developed and structured • verbalise their understanding of how a piece of music functions, develops over time and what it might mean to them and the original composer or performer
Synthesis	Compiling information together in a different way by combining elements in a new pattern or proposing alternative solutions	Build, choose, combine, compile, compose, construct, create, design, develop, estimate, formulate, imagine, invent, make up, originate, plan, predict, propose, solve, solution, suppose, discuss, modify, change, original, improve, adapt, minimise, maximise, delete, theorise, elaborate, test, improve, happen, change	• Using old ideas to create new ones • Generalising from given facts • Relating knowledge from several areas • Predicting, drawing conclusions	Pupils can: • be thoroughly acquainted with the stylistic requirements of a given piece or musical style and can extend these appropriately to construct their own, musically convincing individual interpretation • be highly imaginative within musical composition, originating, inventing and imagining potential musical composition opportunities that draw together knowledge from a range of curriculum areas and theorise about possible musical outcomes or solutions • speculate and theorise about musical meanings, compositional outcomes and performance interpretation, testing theories through the synthesis of ideas into new and divergent solutions
Evaluation	Presenting and defending opinions by making judgements about information, validity of ideas or quality of work based on a set of criteria	Award, choose, conclude, criticise, decide, defend, determine, dispute, evaluate, judge, justify, measure, compare, mark, rate, recommend, rule on, select, agree, interpret, explain, appraise, prioritise, opinion, support, importance, criteria, prove, disprove, assess, influence, perceive, value, estimate, influence, deduct	• Comparison and discrimination between ideas • Assessment of value of theories, presentations • Making choices based on reasoned argument • Verifying value of evidence • Recognising subjectivity	Pupils can: • justify, explain and defend their own musical choices in performance, evaluating and disputing alternative possibilities in the context of musical subjectivity • present their compositional ideas with confidence and show an advanced ability to explain and appraise their own actions in light of others' work or criticism of their own • recognise the subjective nature of musical understanding but show a developed skill to compare, discriminate and value alternative perspectives and understand their grounding in musical evidence

Adapted from Bloom 1956 and from litstudies.org/BloomTaxonomy.htm themselves. As a first step in seeking to establish collaboration between teachers, what follows are a number of short case studies of individual pupils who have been identified as musically talented by their various teachers. Through analysing these we hope that we can begin to obtain a clearer picture of what these pupils can do naturally and what they can go on to achieve through our careful teaching. Each case study is preceded by a paragraph describing the school taken from their most recent Ofsted report.

Case study 1 – Abigail

(Jo Lord, head of music, Middleton Technology College)

Middleton Technology School has 1,073 pupils and numbers have risen in recent years. There are more boys than girls in all years. Pupils are mainly of white United Kingdom background and there are small numbers of pupils of black Caribbean, black African, Asian, Chinese and white European backgrounds. A small number of pupils have English as an additional language, but none are in the early stages of English language acquisition. A very small number of pupils are from refugee and traveller families. The proportion of pupils entitled to free school meals is broadly average and it is falling. The school is in a socially deprived area and one in which levels of unemployment are high. The percentage of pupils with statements of special educational needs is close to average and is rising slowly. The percentage on the school's register of special educational needs is below average. The areas of pupils' needs are mainly for dyslexia, moderate learning difficulties and emotional and behavioural difficulties. Attainment on entry to the school is below average, but it is rising. Pupils' literacy skills are below average and the proportion of higher attaining pupils entering the school is below average. The attainment on entry of the year group of pupils who took their GCSE examinations in 2002 was well below average. The school is a technology school with a city learning centre (CLC) attached. It has recently received beacon school status (Ofsted report, March 2003).

Abigail joined our school in 2000. During her time at primary school she had received limited opportunities to learn about music during classroom time and had not received instrumental lessons or participated in extracurricular activities such as the choir or instrumental ensembles. Her family were very supportive but had not received any formal musical training themselves. Abigail was placed in the top set in Year 7, but was not identified as part of the whole-school gifted and talented cohort.

During her early music lessons in Year 7, Abigail quickly demonstrated natural musical ability. She responded quickly to music, being able to feel and maintain a steady pulse in time with the music. She was able to hear and repeat quite complex rhythmic patterns and play in time with a backing beat on a keyboard, adapting quickly to correct herself if she made a mistake and lost the timing. She was able to sing in tune and maintain parts confidently when singing rounds or within simple two-part class singing. Abigail joined the Year 7 choir and, whilst circulating amongst the choir, it became clear to me that she had a 'special' singing voice. It was clear, confident, in tune and had a lovely, distinctive tone quality.

Abigail was introduced to the singing teacher who helps with the choirs as well as delivering individual and small-group lessons. We spoke to Abigail privately and told her that we thought she had a special talent and that she must continue singing. Throughout Year 7 she sang small solos with the choir and in classroom lessons continued to demonstrate high levels of musical ability, completing extension work and showing musicality in her performances and composition.

Abigail was added to the subject-specific gifted and talented list as being talented in music.

In Year 8 Abigail moved to the senior choir and was given a free individual singing lesson. Normally members of the choir in Years 8 and 9 would receive lessons in small groups. Throughout Years 8 and 9 we continued to encourage Abigail to develop her talents by singing solos at school concerts, open evenings and at the local music festival. She also participated in the steel band but did not want to learn another instrument. In lessons she was encouraged to work independently with other talented students. Her composing work was demonstrating great flair and she was taught about devices to develop her compositions such as sequences, retrograde, imitation and inversion. She was able to understand these and use them effectively in her compositions. When performing for the class she used expression such as dynamics, variations in tempo, and articulation such as staccato and legato. Her listening and appraising work demonstrated an ability to hear details such as musical devices and also to express and justify opinions about the success of a piece of music. Abigail chose music as a GCSE option at the end of Year 9.

Throughout Years 10 and 11 she continued to show great enthusiasm and interest in different types of music. In the classroom she continued to demonstrate the same flair and talent and was now working hard to develop note-reading skills. Her singing technique developed considerably and she was being encouraged to improvise and ornament the popular songs that she was learning. This is a skill that she quickly understood and was able to do naturally. She also started to do some two-part singing with another student. Initially she found this difficult but with perseverance her skills improved. At choir she was a leader in the soprano section, being able to maintain the parts confidently.

When the opportunity to attend a summer school for choral singing at the local music centre arose she was encouraged to take part. I organised lifts for her as it was difficult for her family to take and collect her each day. At the summer school she was selected to perform a piece as part of a small ensemble as well as singing with the whole choir. After the summer school she was encouraged to join the Borough Youth Choir, which she did, and she still attends regularly.

As part of her GCSE coursework she composed a song and used Cubase to compose a backing track for the song. With the help of a technician after school she was also able to record the vocal for the song herself.

The gifted and talented fund supported her throughout school, for example by buying a keyboard for her to borrow during her GCSE studies, by paying for her tickets for trips to the theatre to see musicals and by paying entry fees for her music festival entries.

Abigail completed her GCSE course in 2005 and is predicted an A or A*. She is intending to continue studying music to A level and we have given her considerable guidance as to where she should study at this level. She has been taken on a visit and met the head of music at the educational establishment, as well as their singing teacher. We also discussed the possibility of her receiving piano lessons to help with her studies, particularly her note-reading skills.

With support and encouragement Abigail's talents and enthusiasm have flourished, despite limited experiences early on in life.

A selection of Abigail's work can be found on the accompanying CD. This includes examples of her composition work, a vocal performance from a school concert and a selection of written material from her GCSE coursework.

Case study 2 – Emily

(Richard Lord, head of music, Flixton Girls' High School)

Flixton Girls' High School is a secondary modern school with 1,005 girls aged 11 to 16. Numbers have risen since the last inspection. The great majority of girls are from white United Kingdom backgrounds. There are small numbers each of Indian, Pakistani, Caribbean, Chinese, black African, Bangladeshi, and very small numbers of girls from other ethnic minority backgrounds. The proportion of girls who do not have English as their first language is above average. None is in the early stages of acquiring English language. The percentage of pupils entitled to free school meals is broadly average. The percentage of pupils with statements of special educational needs is below the national average and the percentage of pupils on the school's register of special educational needs is broadly average. Attainment on entry to the school is currently below average and there are fewer higher attaining girls than normally seen. Within the local education authority, 40 per cent of pupils are selected for grammar schools at the age of 11. The level of girls' attainment on entry is rising. The school has been involved in a project with the local authority ethnic minority achievement unit. Buildings are used for community use by Trafford Music Centre and by adult evening classes. The school has been awarded Sportsmark in 2002 and is reapplying to become a sports college (Ofsted report, February 2004).

Every year the most able 30 per cent of pupils in the borough go to grammar schools, and the remainder are distributed to the other schools in the borough. As a result, musically talented pupils nearly always display very specific talents, usually with regard to either composing or performing. This year 76 per cent gained Level 5 or above in music; last year 73 per cent. There are a small number, less than 10 per cent, who gain higher than a Level 5 – this is essentially due to the low starting point many pupils have when they arrive. Approximately 10 per cent of the school's cohort receives instrumental or vocal tuition.

Emily was on the SEN register for a specific learning difficulty (dyslexia) and for behavioural issues. I first encountered her in Year 9, and her only contribution to early lessons was to disrupt them. It finally transpired that Emily was a very talented singer who had recently got through to the final of a national young talent competition.

At this point in time Emily's class work was very poor. She displayed considerable flair with regard to composing, but had no concept of how to organise her work, or how to write extended pieces appropriate to her ability. She would produce short pieces that displayed her obvious ability but she produced no extended work, and would not commit to writing things down. Emily was also completely unable to verbalise her thinking in music due to her specific learning difficulty. But she behaved in a completely instinctive manner, relying upon her ear to guide her.

Emily's singing was based on technical inaccuracy. The only song she would perform was 'My Heart Will Go On' from the film *Titanic*, and she would only sing it using her chest voice. She could sing a range of E below middle C to E above middle C using her chest voice in a forceful way. She would not use her head voice at all. The first thing I persuaded Emily to do was to partake in school activities. Firstly, she became a member of the choir and then we persuaded her to take singing lessons with our singing teacher. This worked wonders with her singing over the remaining three years. By the end of Year 11 she performed three songs beautifully for her GCSE, gaining maximum marks for her performing.

Whilst encouraging her to improve her performing skills was relatively easy, working with the obvious talent and flair she had for composition was much harder. As a fall-back position she would always compose using a simple chord progression, e.g. the almost inevitable I–VI–IV–V progression. In Year 9 this was challenged by making her use non-conventional composing techniques, including chord clusters and chromatic scales, in her compositions. Differentiated worksheets were prepared and, along with other able members of her class, she was given challenging tasks to complete.

In Key Stage 4 Emily really struggled with academic work. She found it very difficult to access this aspect of the course but thrived on practical work. A change of singing teacher was forced upon us and this provided a major stimulus for Emily. He encouraged her to start writing her own songs, one of which we used for her GCSE submission.

At the end of Key Stage 4 there was still a huge difference between Emily's ability to create and perform music and her ability to understand it. It is expected that she will gain a very high grade at GCSE, but only due to the strength of her performing and composing. Her music GCSE grade will be the highest one she gains. Her inability to appraise her work and develop effective briefs, together with an inability to learn and use the language for learning will prevent her from attaining the very highest level. Her specific learning difficulty was a major barrier in this.

Emily is taking a professional performers' course at a college next year. She visited me recently at school to tell me she had reached the final audition rounds of X-Factor, and had been signed by a major agent.

Case study 3 – Gemma

(Richard Lord, head of music, Flixton Girls' High School)

Gemma had had singing lessons since she was 13 and developed an excellent technique. She had not taken music at GCSE because the course had not run for several years due to lack of interest. She came to my attention early in Year 10, whilst rehearsing for a school production. In December 2002 she asked me if it would be possible for her to take music GCSE in her own time.

Gemma stayed after school for between 45 minutes and 1 hour most weeks and initially worked her way through the workbooks I had prepared for other GCSE students. She also started working on her compositions in her own time. She found the most effective way to compose was to write melodically using her vocal skills. Both of her compositions were songs.

She was also a competent keyboard player and had the confidence to experiment with chords. I encouraged her to experiment with her accompaniments and she came up with interesting progressions that improved the quality of her work. Her compositions and performing were awarded full marks.

The hardest part of doing the course in such a limited amount of time was being able to reinforce the learning that took place for the listening exam, so a creative approach was needed. I decided to help her develop her independent learning skills. Using the OCR language for learning and the GCSE specification Gemma researched the areas of study herself. Gemma then used the Rheingold listening exam pack for practice but also used the internet to consolidate her learning. She was given topics to research and revise and researched them on the internet, starting with the BBC's GCSE Bitesize, but moving onto other sites as appropriate. This approach worked extremely well with such a capable student as she produced excellent revision materials for herself and these ideally suited her learning style.

Gemma ultimately achieved a Grade A in her GCSE music.

Case study 4 – Jonathan

(Andy Cope, head of music, Leek Specialist Technology School)

This is a co-educational secondary school, educating children from the age of 13 to 18, one of two in the town. It is smaller than most secondary schools. There are 566 pupils on roll, of whom 123 are in the sixth form. There are more boys than girls. Pupils are drawn from a very large and diverse catchment area, part urban and part rural, including isolated hamlets and farms and containing some areas of social disadvantage. The proportion of pupils entitled to free school meals, just over 12 per cent, is close to average for the country as a whole. The proportion of pupils identified as having special educational needs is also close to average, but the numbers with statements of special educational needs, identified as having more serious needs, is above average. Almost all the pupils are white, although the school does have the advantage of a small number of pupils who represent other world cultures. For less than 1 per cent of pupils English is an additional language, which is below the average nationally. The attainment of pupils on entry to the school is below average, overall, but is improving steadily (Ofsted report, October 2000).

Jonathan came to LHS from Churnet View Middle School. He was identified as being musically talented before arriving by both peripatetic staff and his previous head of music. He had lessons on French horn (grade 4 now 5) with the school peripatetic teacher and private piano lessons (grade 6 now 7/8). His previous music teacher passed on some samples of his composing work to me. I examined these carefully.

During his first few weeks at Leek High School, and in order to extend his piano and horn skills, Jonathan was selected to accompany students in the December concert, perform on the horn within a selected ensemble and contribute a piano solo. The same has applied to each concert since he has been here. He has also been actively involved in providing piano music at awards ceremonies, school open evenings, etc. Involvement in concerts has led to Jonathan receiving a number of awards in piano playing and accompanying.

In subsequent terms, Jonathan has been given other special tasks and responsibilities such as arranging pop tunes for electronic keyboard for use by beginner and intermediate pupils within school music lessons.

Jonathan was encouraged to take GCSE music and discussions have already been held about A level choices. In composing work, Jonathan has been given personal attention according to his needs. He has been given detailed tasks including learning about jazz harmony and modernist techniques such as serialism. His GCSE compositions had been gradually developed into an A standard by the end of the second term. Through discussions with Jonathan, I have explained the need to move into more complex ideas that could be incorporated into A level work – thus giving him a much better chance of attaining an A grade at A level and indeed towards a future, possible career in music.

Case study 5 – John

(Andy Cope, head of music, Leek Specialist Technology School)

Churnet View Middle School did not identify John as gifted and talented. He did not have formal lessons at school but was partly self-taught and partly taught by his father, who is a local rock musician. In discussions with the class I discovered that John already played the guitar and sang. After arranging for John to perform to me, I decided that he was a musically talented student. In the three years that John was at Leek High School, I encouraged him to become actively involved in much extracurricular music-making besides personally teaching him much about the guitar. These opportunities included performing in school concerts as a soloist and in rock bands, and he won many awards as a result.

I arranged for John to have singing lessons at school and, as a result, John won through to the finals of the esteemed Staffordshire County Pop Stars competition. I also trained him to help teach younger pupils how to play the guitar in the school guitar club.

John was encouraged to take GCSE music. In his composition work he was encouraged to experiment with new ways of composing music for the guitar, particularly in embellishing chords, and in writing three-part vocal textures, etc. He achieved full marks in his performing and composing coursework. John has himself become influential in encouraging music-making in others. His highly musical active time at school has encouraged him to form bands both in and out of school, in which he himself takes a leading role.

I also noticed John's interest in engineering and gave him many opportunities and assignments in maintaining guitars, amps and other equipment through which he has developed many practical skills.

Case study 6 – Stuart

(Andy Cope, head of music, Leek Specialist Technology School)

Stuart was a student who had not taken any interest in music before coming to high school. After a course of classroom guitar lessons during the first half term, I identified Stuart as being musically talented by spotting the potential inherent in his early stages of his learning/playing. During a visit to one lesson from the headteacher of the school, I selected Stuart from the class to perform what he had learnt to the headteacher in order to single him out as being special. He relished the opportunity with confidence and a big smile!

Stuart very quickly learnt guitar skills. I provided him with bass guitar lessons and he had soon booked himself private lessons with a bass guitar teacher. He was soon playing extensive and complex pieces in a mature way. After three years of learning, he is now in demand as a bass player with older, more established musicians and regularly serves a number of local bands playing blues, jazz and rock.

Stuart was encouraged to take GCSE music. In his composition work he was given much encouragement and direction in experimenting with new and unusual techniques such as double-handed tapping and palm rubs, etc. He achieved full marks in his performing and composing coursework and is now preparing for A level music. I asked Stuart to take on the role of school bass teacher. He did this and learned much from the experience – as is already established, a person learns much from teaching others, therefore this is used at the high school as a means of developing musically talented pupils wherever possible.

Case study 7 – Richard

(Pat Calcutt, head of music, Bedford High School)

Bedford High is a mixed, larger than average comprehensive school for pupils aged 11 to 16. The number of pupils on roll is 1,201 (boys 613; girls 588). Relatively few pupils are from socially advantaged homes. The school was an amalgamation of a boys' grammar and a mixed secondary modern; consequently it is situated on two sites approximately 200 metres apart. There are very low numbers of pupils from a minority ethnic background or having English as a second language. The number of pupils on the special educational needs register is above average as is the number of pupils eligible for free school meals. The number of pupils with a statement of special educational need is also above average. Most of these pupils have learning difficulties but a substantial number have behavioural difficulties. Overall, standards of attainment on entry are below average. The school successfully acquired Business and Enterprise status in September 2003. Another successful feature is the school's involvement with the Construction Industry Training Board (CITB), which has its own facility on site (Ofsted report, September 2004).

In Year 7 Richard was a quiet pupil who was well behaved. His written work was average and he was achieving the expected level for his age. He participated and cooperated in practical group work but never stood out as being particularly talented until towards the end of Year 8. The class was asked to compose, in groups, a samba composition including some call and response. Richard was able to lead the group confidently by singing the call with a strong and pleasing voice as well as holding the group together with a strong and regular drumbeat. This was the first time he had sung solo and we realised that there was a lot of potential. He was encouraged to join the school choir and was able to sing confidently holding his own part in SAB. He volunteered to sing at a Christmas concert and began to have guitar lessons in school.

He was chosen to attend a workshop for gifted and talented pupils working with the new software (Cubase SX) the school had just purchased. He was then asked to support other pupils on this software. Again, he enjoyed this challenge and as a result he has been involved in a music technology club that runs weekly after school. More recently, he was chosen to take the lead role in the school production of *'Grease'*, proving that he was not only talented musically but also a very competent actor. In Year 11, he took on another lead role in *'Blood Brothers'*, which was a much more demanding role in terms of acting and singing and again he rose to the challenge (listen to his solo performance on the accompanying CD). His guitar playing is quite outstanding and he has also taught himself to play the ukulele, again performing in the school concert. He has performed as singer and guitarist in the school soul band as well as performing with other rock bands. Richard has been studying GCSE music for the last two years and he is expected to achieve a high grade. He is planning to follow a performing arts course at college.

There is a selection of Richard's work including composition work done for his recent GCSE on the accompanying CD. Richard has also provided examples of his solo and ensemble performances together with a very innovative integrated assignment.

Common features of musically talented pupils from the case studies

The table opposite draws together the findings from these seven pupil case studies. It compiles the information relating to the history of each pupil's musical experiences and the characteristics they exhibited that led to their identification. This table will be extended in following chapters as we begin to see how these teachers sought to meet the educational needs of these musically talented pupils.

Analysis of case study materials

Pupil	History	Identification
Abigail	• Limited opportunities • Supportive family but no musical training • Not identified as G&T on entry	• Feel and maintain a steady pulse • Hear and repeat complex rhythms • Play in time with a backing track on a keyboard • Correct mistakes • Readjust timing • Sing in tune and maintain part singing confidently • 'Special' singing voice: clear, confident, distinctive tone • Compositional flair • Effective use of compositional devices (e.g. dynamic and tempo variations, expressive articulation) • Detailed observations in listening exercises • Able to express and justify musical opinions
Emily	• SEN register for dyslexia and behavioural issues • Finalist in national talent competition • Lack of organisational skills • Lack of commitment to writing things down • Unable to verbalise her thinking	• Compositional flair • Talented singer
Gemma	• Excellent singer	• Identified during rehearsals for school production in Year 10 • Excellent singing technique
Jonathan	• Previously identified as musically talented by staff at middle school • French horn and piano player	• Identified through collaboration with staff at middle school • Examination of composition work done at Key Stage 2/3
John	• Taught guitar by father	• Observation of guitar playing and singing
Stuart	• No previous musical experience or apparent interest	• Potential instrumental ability on the guitar spotted early during class sessions • Confidence and enthusiasm in performing for others
Richard		• Leadership qualities • Strong vocal lead • Strong rhythmic ability

Drawing on the case study materials supplied by teachers, government materials (including those within the National Curriculum and Excellence in Cities initiative) and other relevant research (such as Bloom's taxonomy discussed above), it is possible to draw up a framework of potential features that musically talented pupils will exhibit, a summary of which is also shown overleaf.

Having identified these features, teachers make use of a range of devices to help document the abilities of their musically talented pupils. Common devices include checklists of questions such as those illustrated in Appendix 3.1 provided by Nottingham City LEA. Other strategies that teachers adopt link identification with provision. Examples of this can been seen in the individual education plans for Darren and Vicky that we discussed in Chapter 2 and which we will revisit again in Chapter 4.

Features of a musically talented pupil

Early identification features	
General	<ul><li>Feeling and maintaining a steady pulse</li><li>Finding it difficult not to respond to music in some way</li><li>Hearing and repeating complex rhythms</li><li>Memorising music quickly without any apparent effort</li><li>Captivated by sounds</li><li>Often responding physically to music</li><li>Making music spontaneously inside and outside the classroom</li><li>Potential leadership qualities</li></ul>
Vocally	<ul><li>Natural singing ability, being able to sing in tune and maintain a part confidently</li><li>Demonstrating a special singing voice that may be clear, confident and possess a distinctive tone</li><li>Singing and playing music with a natural awareness of the musical phrase</li></ul>
Performing	<ul><li>Confidence and enthusiasm in performance</li><li>Selecting an instrument carefully and being reluctant to relinquish it</li><li>Playing in time with a backing track, readjusting timing if required</li></ul>
Composing	<ul><li>Demonstrating the ability to communicate through music, with expression, feeling and confidence</li><li>Showing strong preferences, single-mindedness and a sustained inner drive to make music</li><li>Ability to express and justify musical opinions</li></ul>
Listening/appraising	<ul><li>Detailed observations in listening exercises</li></ul>
Later identification features/avenues for possible developments	
Performing	<ul><li>Accuracy in performance</li><li>Demonstrating a range of possible musical interpretations</li><li>Drawing lessons from various different performance opportunities and applying these constructively within a new performance context</li><li>Understanding, appreciating and seeking to convey their own musical interpretation of a given piece</li><li>Being thoroughly acquainted with the stylistic requirements of a given musical style and extending these appropriately to construct their own, musically convincing individual interpretation</li><li>Justifying, explaining and defending their own musical choices in performance</li></ul>
Composing	<ul><li>Composing with flair often beyond given instructions, outlining and inferring possible compositional opportunities within a given style</li><li>Showing an extensive flair for freely experimenting, improvising and developing musical ideas within a composition project and organising these into a coherent whole, justifying their choices throughout</li><li>Showing a clearly analytical approach to musical composition and developing an understanding of how musical ideas are generated, developed and structured</li><li>Being highly imaginative within musical composition, originating, inventing and imagining potential musical opportunities that draw together knowledge from a range of curriculum areas and theorising about possible musical outcomes or solutions</li><li>Presenting compositional ideas with confidence and showing an advanced ability to explain and appraise their own actions in light of others' work or criticism of their own</li></ul>
Listening/appraising	<ul><li>Grasping musical meanings within listening activities and translating these meanings across a range of contexts</li><li>Responding to music in an imaginative way, applying musical knowledge and understanding in unusual ways</li><li>Verbalising their understanding of how a piece of music functions, develops over time and what it might mean to them and the original composer or performer</li><li>Speculating and theorising about musical meanings, compositional outcomes and performance interpretation</li><li>Testing theories through the synthesis of ideas into new and divergent solutions</li><li>Recognising the subjective nature of musical understanding but showing a developed skill to compare, discriminate and value alternative perspectives and understand their grounding in musical evidence</li></ul>

Whole-school and departmental processes for identifying musically talented pupils

As we have discussed in Chapter 2, it will be important for the music teacher to have a close working relationship with the G&T coordinator in order to identify those pupils who are musically talented or more generally gifted in other areas of the curriculum.

There is no one single method of identification that will be entirely accurate. It will be necessary to use a range of methods and collect an assortment of data about pupils in order to make an informed judgement. These methods can be divided into two main categories:

1. Identifying musically talented pupils through a range of recognised and probably pre-established means, and then making specific provision for their needs; or

2. Providing all pupils with a range of challenging musical opportunities that will reveal their potential musical talents.

In practice, these two approaches will overlap and interlink. What music teachers need to develop is a process that draws on established procedures as well as new opportunities in order to identify the musically talented in any given cohort of pupils. On the next page is a list of common methods, together with a brief analysis of their strengths and limitations.

Developing baseline assessment as a tool for identifying musically talented pupils

The following section reports on a somewhat unique experiment in baseline assessment in music conducted by all the high schools in Wigan LEA. It has been written by Will Evans, who is currently senior lecturer in music education at the Institute of Education, Manchester Metropolitan University. At the time, he was head of music at one of the high schools involved in the experiment, Fred Longworth High School in Tyldesley. As the case study unfolds, it will be seen that a joined-up approach to baseline assessment between a group of local schools can be a tremendously useful tool in helping teachers identify those pupils who are truly musically talented.

Introduction

Every year music teachers face the wonderful opportunity of meeting a new cohort of pupils. Almost immediately that these pupils enter our classrooms we are asked to assess their abilities and predict their musical and academic futures. Many of the pupils, as we know, come from varying backgrounds. Their experiences of music within Key Stages 1 and 2 will be diverse. Many will have

Strengths and limitations of other identification methods

Method	Strengths	Limitations
National Curriculum tests	Judged against school curriculum. Measure of longitudinal progress.	High levels of achievement dependent on access to appropriate curriculum opportunities.
Ability profile tests	Useful screening procedure. Objective evaluation of performance on certain skills in comparison with others of similar age. Relatively inexpensive.	Only able to give information on the limited range of skills measured. Usually limited to measuring analytic skills and do not reward divergent thinking. May not identify pupils with different cultural/linguistic backgrounds or dyslexic pupils. Format may be daunting for some pupils. Less robust at the extremes of the range.
National Curriculum teacher assessment	Based on clear criteria. Linked to the school curriculum.	High levels of achievement dependent on access to appropriate curriculum opportunities. Open to interpretation.
Teacher nomination	Makes use of teacher's ongoing assessments of pupils. Closely linked to provision. Facilitates recognition of pupils' responses to teaching, levels of initiative and interest, lateral thinking and extent of high-level problem solving.	Subjective if not undertaken against agreed criteria. Clearly linked to generality of practice. Relies on teaching approaches which are confident, challenging and flexible.
Classroom observation	May help to confirm other assessments through systematic data collection based on agreed criteria. Assesses child in familiar context doing familiar tasks.	Time-consuming and therefore expensive. Can be subjective if not undertaken rigorously and on a series of occasions.
Examination of pupil work	Good measure of written outcomes. Helps refine teacher expectations through analysis of high-quality work.	Can be subjective if not undertaken rigorously. Only measures achievement not potential. High performance reliant on good opportunities and high teacher expectation. Over-reliance on written work can hide wider potential.
Subject-specific checklists	Useful in assisting teachers to explore ability in their subject and thereby recognise those with high ability. Discussion generated in departments can serve to facilitate curriculum design.	Checklists cannot be relevant for each individual. Extensive lists can be unwieldy to manage and time-consuming to administer.
Generic checklists	Easily accessible. Simple to handle.	Can run the risk of creating stereotypes. Too general to be useful in curriculum terms. Validity remains questionable.
Reading tests	Easy to administer. Reading competence gives some indication of likely exam performance.	Reading is a skill rather than an ability and high scores on reading tests are not a reliable indicator of cognitive ability.
Creativity tests	Measures abilities not normally assessed as part of school assessment. Offers divergent thinkers a chance to display their ability.	Time-consuming to administer. Validity remains questionable.
Educational psychologists	Invaluable in identifying high ability linked to complex issues, e.g. areas of SEN.	Time-consuming and expensive. Unnecessary for most gifted pupils.
Parents and peers	Intimate knowledge of the individual. Can take account of performance outside school environment.	Subjective, based on own experience and knowledge.

engaged in very little study of music. But some pupils will have very advanced musical skills and be confident singers, instrumentalists, composers or listeners. For many pupils music will be an important part of their life outside of school. They will listen to music with their friends, dance to it at parties and discos, learn the lyrics of their favourite songs and perform at karaokes. The musical lives of many 11- and 12-year-olds are fairly diverse. This is a tremendous challenge for us as teachers. How can we harness any natural talents, nurtured and developed musical skills or general interest within our lessons?

We are, of course, given considerable amounts of data drawn from tests outside our main discipline. We are asked to draw opinions, set targets and analyse this data to help plan our teaching and inform our curriculum development. Long may the argument continue to rage about the usefulness of this data. But it only gives us part of the ammunition that we need to understand the complexity of the situation that we face.

As all this happens we struggle to do the real work of teaching in the classroom, developing new ways of introducing pupils to musical and learning experiences whilst integrating the latest governmental, school or musical initiative. We struggle to learn names and faces and normally find ourselves learning the names of those who demand our attention rather than deserve it. But it is vital to introduce Year 7 pupils positively to music as a subject in the Key Stage 3 curriculum and to get them all enthused. It is crucial to have a system that assesses their musical skills and identifies the potentially musically talented pupils as early as possible.

Perhaps focusing on a few simple ideas can help us as teachers. Firstly, looking at each new class and realising that between 5 and 10 per cent should be musically talented will be a good starting point. In these early lessons we have the opportunity to look very positively at the new classes we get. Of course, there is the challenge of how we will 'spot' their musical talents. Too often we can take the easy road out of this predicament and identify the talented performer. But how should we identify the potential composer, or the pupil with perfect pitch or an aptitude for listening activities? We should recognise that there are many external factors that will affect and influence these choices. For example, the adoption of new technologies within music education has changed the nature and function of teaching and learning. What will or should the music classroom of the twenty-first century look like? Within these classrooms what skills or abilities will the musically talented pupil have? Will they be the same as the musical attributes of pupils in previous generations?

Our experiments with baseline assessment

One solution that we, as a group of music teachers within Fred Longworth High School, discovered was the use of a baseline assessment mechanism to help identify musically talented pupils. In fact, it was a useful tool for assessing all pupils at the very beginning of Year 7. But through this mechanism, and by considering other external data, musically talented pupils could be identified too.

It was important for us to develop a way of baseline testing that moved away from just looking at obvious skills such as performance ability or the Bentley Test and looked at combined musical activities. It was also a good chance to make assessment work for us as teachers rather than just being something that was 'bolted on' to the end of a scheme of work. The constant 'assessment culture' within the school needed taming within our music department. Part of this process was adapting it to help, rather than hinder, our work as teachers.

After much deliberation we realised that we needed a scheme of work that would allow pupils to show what they knew and why they knew it. A simple standardised test was never going to be enough as this would probably be far more limited by the pupils' academic ability rather than their musical skills and talents. The baseline test we finally worked with was developed from the first suggested unit of Curriculum 2000. It was developed in conjunction with several other leading teachers from Wigan schools and implemented across high schools within the LEA. We decided to allow pupils to work through a project whilst, at the same time, building in a way to assess their 'base' level in each core musical skill. It was obvious that as the pupils did this they would begin to improve, but it would at least give us a chance to look at this work within a set framework that could inform our future planning.

As we began to do this we realised that there were other skills and signs that began to 'flag up' potentially musically talented pupils. We realised that improvisation became an important intricate and linking concept which, when included as an integral part of our educational practice, gave us a real chance to very quickly assess pupils' intuitive reaction to musical concepts. Early classroom work on clapping games, rhythm exercises and melodic memory gave us a real opportunity to begin to baseline assess the pupils' musical ability. The link between improvisation and musical ability is fascinating and there is certainly a lot more work to be done. The working limits of a 5–10 per cent musically talented cohort in each class gave us a very positive approach to these lessons.

Broadening the net: linking music with other areas of achievement

Developing an approach to baseline assessment helped us to begin to reconsider what we meant by pupils being musically talented. One of the implications of this for our pupils' work in our classrooms was that we found ourselves becoming more open in respect of the characteristics or abilities that these pupils should display. This led us naturally to consider the links between musical learning itself and what other things pupils might learn through studying music.

When we looked at individual cases within our school it was certainly true that musically talented pupils were often able in many other areas of the curriculum. We were able to differentiate within this group by those pupils who were strong across many musical disciplines and those who had more limited or focused musical skills. The pupils who were strong across many musical disciplines – e.g. performing, composing and listening – seemed to be the pupils who were also able in many other subjects.

There was a smaller core of pupils, often harder to spot, who were more likely to be talented in one specific musical area. These pupils often seemed to have a heightened musical ability in a specific part of the curriculum, often performing or composing, but this was not matched with all-round skill. Due to this lack of overall academic prowess it was far easier for these pupils to slip through the net. Within music lessons, they could quickly become disaffected if the lesson focused on concepts or practices outside their specific area of expertise or talent. These pupils shared a number of common characteristics. They had a single-minded way of working that often came across in an almost obsessive manner. They seemed interested in learning certain aspects of performance or composing to a very high level but this would often exclude many others. This made them very interesting pupils to teach and even more interesting pupils to plan a curriculum for! For these pupils, we found that the balance between learning in music and through it became crucial. They were certainly very interested in learning certain musical skills but there was no drive to understand other linked concepts or even a drive to achieve in an overall sense within the subject.

Within the arts provision across the school, we developed several ideas that we hoped would help all pupils to learn in a more integrated manner. One of the key ideas was what became known as Intervention Lessons in the Arts. For several years within Wigan LEA the ARTS (Arts, Reasoning and Thinking Skills) project had developed a set of thirty such lessons, ten in each of the subject areas of music, art and drama. The idea of these lessons was to look at pupils' cognitive acceleration in and through the use of arts lessons. This work built on a belief that the arts deal with many higher order thinking skills, which other subjects cannot do in such a natural manner. But there had been little focus on what these skills were and even less on how to concentrate work in arts lessons upon them. The ARTS project aim was to focus pupils' work on thinking skills and hopefully move their progression forwards at an accelerated rate.

These lessons gave a perfect opportunity for all pupils to learn through, and about, their own thinking processes. They focused on learning more than just music by teaching pupils to learn and think for themselves. The programme gave them an opportunity to think through what they were learning in school and how working in each subject (and especially the arts) could benefit other aspects of their academic work. It seemed particularly useful in developing musically talented pupils and certainly helped pupils with specific musical talents to apply their skills to the rest of the subject and school life in general.

If nothing else, having to consider the needs of musically talented pupils in school certainly made us consider new ideas. The process of identifying, working with and planning for musically talented pupils initiated many ideas that benefited all the pupils that we taught. It also made us try to make closer links between areas of the music curriculum and other curriculum subjects within the school.

Using strategies to provide for musically talented pupils is a very positive way of showing how to plan and differentiate for pupils' individual needs. It gives a chance to directly monitor pupils who are identified at an early stage as being talented and allows us to easily reflect upon our classroom work and analyse how we improve our practice.

The government's gifted and talented initiative may eventually be subsumed into a new one. What won't change is the need for us to tailor the music curriculum to the individual needs of the pupils sitting in front of us day by day. Pupils' skills, abilities and talents in music will become increasingly diverse. Any strategy that allows us to focus upon the positives and identify pupils who show talent for music will only be to our advantage.

Epilogue

In 2003 Dylan Mills, also known as Dizzee Rascal, was announced as the winner of the 2003 Mercury Music Prize. His album *Boy in Da Corner* was released earlier to rave reviews across the world. The album's title was autobiographical. It was about his expulsion from two high schools in East London. In his words, 'I'd been that kid in the corner of the classroom, the street corner. I had my back against the wall in general' (Ojumu 2003: 48). In a fascinating piece in *The Observer*, Mills discussed the influence of his music teacher, Tim Smith, and the music department on his work:

> There were good facilities in the music department, which is why I liked it and it was the only place in the school that I actually wanted to be. I was in the back room of the music department most of the time, working alone. I was focused and I didn't worry about what else was going on. I played music as I'd always imagined hearing it in my head.
>
> School would have been pretty dead really for me without music. Everything started there. I don't really class myself as a musician, I can make music but I'm not the greatest technically.
>
> I got on with Tim Smith from the start. He just let me get on with things. I'm never going to forget him. I'm not like that.
>
> (Ojumu 2003: 48)

And what did Tim Smith have to say about Dylan Mills and his work?

> I try to let students do what they want. I aim to create an atmosphere where they feel safe and can experiment. Dylan knew what he wanted to achieve and he worked quickly. His music had a clear structure and pattern, an amazing balance between rhythm, bass and melody.
>
> I'm fortunate to teach arts – you have a real opportunity to work closely with pupils. You can develop a one-to-one relationship that is quite unique.
>
> (Ojumu 2003: 48)

Dylan and Tim's story reflects what is really important in music education today. The effective identification and support of musically talented pupils depends, above all, on the quality of the individual teacher and their relationships with their pupils. Tim Smith managed to provide the time and space for Dylan Mills to find his creative potential and express it through the medium of technology.

Similarly, Alex, discussed at the opening of this chapter, is an inspiration and challenge for us as teachers. His path towards fulfilment of his dreams was hard, but now he says that he:

> treats music as a very good friend. It's something that's helped me to communicate with people, to express myself. It's a language that helps you relate to people. It transcends limitations.
>
> (Alex, during interview, 2003)

The 'system' of school-based education put many obstacles in his way. Formality and orthodoxy were, at times, his invincible opponents. Yet his creative spirit won through. At 29 he believes in himself as a musician and is still moving onwards down his road of discovery.

Embodied in the work of Alex, and demonstrated in the working relationship between Dylan and Tim, is a vision of music education for the twenty-first century. The identification and support of musically talented pupils will require teachers to recognise, acknowledge and support pupils' skills and abilities in a wide range of settings, both within the classroom and beyond the school boundaries into the musical lives of pupils.

Summary

- Musically talented pupils will exhibit an array of musical abilities. Simplistic approaches to identifying these pupils will lead to many being excluded.

- Those pupils defined as being musically talented may well evidence general characteristics of talent, but for some the talent may be exhibited solely in the area of music.

- There are many systems for identifying musically talented pupils, but possibly the best system is sharing judgements, viewpoints and evidence with other local teachers.

- By working constructively with the G&T coordinator, the head of music will be able to draw on a range of methods to help identify the musically talented pupil.

- What teachers define as musical talent will vary, but a general list of features has been supplied that will help teachers structure a range of devices to assist their identification process.

CHAPTER 4

Classroom provision

- What are the foundational principles of the music curriculum?
- How should we consider the curriculum in relation to musically talented pupils?
- Designing a curriculum for musically talented pupils will require teachers to examine their practice before, during and after teaching
- Assessment for learning has a vital role to play in supporting the work of musically talented pupils
- Concepts of classification and framing will help teachers analyse their practice and build opportunities for pupils to engage in musical encounters

In previous chapters we have looked at the importance of departmental policy in relation to musically talented pupils (Chapter 2) and processes by which teachers will be able to identify musically talented pupils (Chapter 3). This chapter moves the issue forward into the classroom and the provision that teachers should make for their musically talented pupils.

Introduction

Elliot Eisner may have done more than any recent thinker to expand and develop notions of arts education and curriculum development. In one of his recent books (Eisner 2002), a chapter entitled 'Visions and Versions of Arts Education' seeks to describe some of the common aims and content of arts education programmes common in schools today. He states clearly that there is no 'sacrosanct vision of the aims of arts education' and that 'examples of diversity abound' (Eisner 2002: 25). However, his summary of the five principles of arts education can be useful starting points as we begin to consider how we will provide for the needs of musically talented pupils.

Eisner's first principle is that music education should give pride of place to what is distinctive about the contemporary musical practice. In other words, music education should keep up to date. It should look to widen the opportunities for all pupils to engage in music beyond music education's traditional approaches. This might include embracing the obvious technological changes that have revolutionised many approaches to the teaching of performance and composition. But it also means that as teachers we have to understand, acknowledge and appreciate the wider world of musical activities from which pupils come from into our classrooms. Musically talented pupils may have particularly well developed musical histories that teachers will have to know about in order to provide for their particular needs within classroom teaching. A snapshot from such a history has been provided in Appendix 2.2.

The second principle that Eisner develops in his vision for an arts education fit for the twenty-first century is related to the nature of intelligence. Picking up on themes drawn from the work of Howard Gardner, he believes that the music curriculum should try to foster the growth of musical intelligence: 'Ability in art is assigned to talent; ability in "intellectual subjects" is assigned to intelligence' (Eisner 2002: 43). As we will be seeing in Chapter 5, intelligence takes many forms. Here it is enough to state that intelligence belongs to the music just as much as to any other part of the curriculum. It is not good enough to say that pupils succeed in music solely on the basis of being musically talented. Talent and intelligence are intertwined and developed in tandem as a result of careful teaching. Intelligent evaluation and reflection on the process of creation should be a common theme in all our pupils' work in music.

Thirdly, Eisner suggests that a key aim of music education is to teach pupils how to create and experience the aesthetic. His disposition is towards an approach to teaching the arts in which the discrete art forms 'can, and probably in most situations will, be addressed in an integrated fashion' (Eisner 2002: 43–4). An example of this in recent work has included the Sound2Picture and Sound2Game teaching resources (www.sound2picture.net and www.sound2game.net) within which the presentation of concepts drawn from the work of a professional sound designer allowed pupils to jointly consider aspects of visual and musical significance and investigate their relationships within composition projects for film and computer games.

More widely, the QCA's recent consultation (Futures – Meeting the Challenge) has many interesting points of departure for arts educators. Not least is the challenge to explore and utilise the potential of new technologies to link subject areas within the curriculum in new ways:

> In a technology-rich world we need to review and modernise what and how we learn. Imagine how a graphic designer works today compared with 30 years ago. What should a modernised music, art or design curriculum be like? . . . They may use technology as a tool for thinking, making or doing. Technology needs to be used more effectively to help develop learners' enquiry skills, logical reasoning, analytical thinking and creativity. It should support individualised and independent learning, while encouraging wider communication and collaborative learning.
>
> (QCA 2005)

The QCA promote the use of technology as a 'force for change' in developing an arts curriculum fit for the twenty-first century. It is clear from recent QCA statements that such 'joined-up curriculum thinking' should be a priority as teachers not only seek to develop artistic skills but also concentrate on the more general development of pupils' creativity, thinking skills and ability to communicate and collaborate. Many of these will be points that we return to in Chapter 5 when we consider how we can best support the learning of musically talented pupils.

Eisner's fourth point states that music education should help pupils recognise what is personal, distinctive and unique about themselves. Hopefully all music educators could agree that a pupil's personal response to a piece of music, song or soundtrack is the key to unlocking their own creative work and to developing their musical understanding. The ability to create engaging starting points and educational situations in which pupils can imbue their personality, character and creative spirit are a vital skill for teachers.

Finally, Eisner relates teaching and learning in the arts to the generation of pupils' alternative views of the world. He insists that art education programmes should make special efforts to enable pupils to secure aesthetic forms of experience in everyday life: 'Each subject studied in schools affords the student a distinctive window or frame through which the world can be viewed' (Eisner 2002: 45).

Our focus has shifted towards the larger issues that music educators hope to address. Eisner's work is a helpful overview of what we should be trying to achieve in our music education curriculum. Just as these things should frame our work with musically talented pupils they are, of course, equally applicable to all pupils under our care. Other educational thinkers have done more specific and focused work that helps us consider the following question in more detail: what sort of music curriculum should we be providing to ensure that all musically talented pupils fulfil their potential?

Curriculum concepts

In order to answer this important question it is necessary to examine precisely what we believe the music curriculum should be for musically talented pupils. There are a number of different curriculum models that we could consider. One will be briefly examined here.

Van Tassell-Baska's (1998) helpful overview of curriculum requirement for the gifted and talented pupil contains four main points concerning level, pace, complexity and depth. Each of these relates closely to how teachers will effectively differentiate the curriculum, thereby accommodating the particular needs of the musically talented pupil.

Level of the curriculum

The level of the curriculum relates to the way in which it will interest and challenge the musically talented pupil. It will be necessary for the music teacher to carefully consider the nature of the curriculum content and how it is presented in various teaching and learning activities.

Pace of the curriculum

The pace at which the curriculum is offered to all pupils is important and an integral part of effective differentiation. For the musically talented pupil, the pace at which the content of the curriculum is presented and the opportunity to engage with the challenges of the associated activities will need to be adjusted appropriately by the teacher.

Complexity of the curriculum

The complexity of the curriculum offered to a musically talented pupil should reflect the capacity of that pupil to engage in advanced levels of musical ideas and activities. For these pupils, it may well be the case that they can handle simultaneous rather than linear processing of ideas, something that we will be considering in respect of effective planning below. It may be that some of the later identification features/avenues for possible developments areas identified within the table on page 58 may be particularly relevant in engendering an appropriate level of complexity for musically talented pupils.

Depth of the curriculum

Finally, in Van Tassell-Baska's model the depth of the curriculum relates to the opportunity of allowing gifted and talented pupils to continue exploring an area of interest to higher levels, perhaps even reaching the level of an expert in a particular field of enquiry.

Van Tassell-Baska's overview of the curriculum principles for gifted and talented learners is a useful starting point for this discussion on how teachers should provide opportunities for musically talented pupils in their classrooms.

Van Tassell-Baska's model applied to the teaching of musically talented pupils

Van Tassell-Baska's model is a useful starting point for teachers as they devise appropriate strategies for teaching musically talented pupils. The table overleaf conceptualises and highlights some of the main points of application. Each of Van Tassell-Baska's points can relate to the three stages of a teacher's work: prior to teaching, during teaching and after teaching. These stages will provide the structure for an extended discussion of how teachers can teach musically talented pupils. Please remember that the teaching of these pupils should always take place within a culture of excellence where all pupils are able to succeed and fulfil their potential in this subject.

Curriculum models for musically talented pupils

Stage	Main features of curriculum models
Before teaching *Planning for level, complexity, pace and depth*	The wider context of music education Effective planning Setting challenging learning objectives and target-setting Designing appropriate teaching activities Pre-lesson rehearsals
During teaching *Moderating level, complexity, pace and depth*	Artistry in teaching: ● The centrality of musical practices in the classroom ● The integration of curriculum elements in the classroom ● The embodied musician as teacher in the classroom ● Freedom and restraint: extension in depth and enrichment in breadth Assessment for learning and the musically talented
After teaching *Revising level, pace, complexity and depth*	The role of summative assessment (or assessment of learning) Ipsative and self-assessment Assessment of teaching

Before teaching

The wider context of music education

All music teaching and learning takes place in a wider context than the classroom. As we have seen when thinking about how we identify those pupils that are musically talented, it is vital to ensure that everything teachers do within the classroom takes account of the wider musical lives that pupils have beyond the classroom. It will be important to collect this information in a systematic way.

Some schools, for example Longdendale Community Language College (see the case study at the end of this chapter), will conduct formal interviews with pupils as a result of responses gathered through a questionnaire completed by form groups on entry to the school in Year 7. Where good relationships exist between schools there may well be detailed information about musically talented pupils being passed through formal channels of communication. In what could be considered exemplary practice in Case Study 4 (see Chapter 3), Jonathan's work from his middle school was passed up to the head of music at Leek Specialist Technology School for examination. This sharing of a portfolio of pupil work, perhaps through an electronic medium, seems like a particularly worthwhile venture and one that we have sought to develop in providing some examples of musically talented pupils' work on the accompanying CD. In another example of good collaborative practice, within one LEA all the high schools collaborated together to baseline assess the entire Year 7 cohort across the authority (see the close of Chapter 3). This gave heads of music in individual schools a much greater awareness of their own pupils' strengths and weaknesses in relation to the other schools in the local area. Either way, it is vital that there is enough information about the prior musical experiences of your pupils for you to be able to plan lessons and schemes of work effectively.

Effective planning

Effective planning is the most important part of good preparation and successful teaching. It will be crucial to ensure that all planning takes account of the identified needs of musically talented pupils. From the case study materials it seems apparent that this can be conducted in two ways.

Firstly, it will be important for teachers to plan in a general way for the provision of musically talented pupils in their classes. This can be conceptualised around the principles of extension and enrichment. One teacher identified extension as being related to the 'depth of engagement' within a teaching and learning activity; enrichment was defined as being a greater 'opportunity of engagement' perhaps beyond the immediate classroom context. The difference between these two different yet complementary approaches can be seen in the 2003/4 audit of talented provision provided by Kingsdown High School (in conjunction with Wigan LEA) on page 31. This clear charting of extension and enrichment opportunities across the Key Stage 3 curriculum is excellent practice and gives a general but useful focus for the more individualised development plans that musically talented pupils will require. The use of target-setting or individual education plans (IEPs) by several of the case study schools was a notable feature of their work. The examples of Darren and Vicky, provided by Kingsdown High School, have been discussed already in Chapter 2.

The structure of these IEPs for Darren and Vicky seem particularly effective. A simple checklist of typical characteristics for musically talented pupils is followed by general opportunities for extending their work. Following this, the teacher has the opportunity to note down comments tailored individually to the musically talented pupil. It should be noted, again, that this teacher has taken the opportunity to describe particular extra-musical issues relating to Darren's behaviour when faced with new musical concepts and the need for Vicky to remain motivated throughout music lessons. The analysis of their particular musical talents, together with other influencing factors, leads to the formation of the actual development plan that staff and pupils can work to throughout the academic year.

Setting challenging learning objectives and target-setting

The setting of learning objectives is a vital part of planning for the effective teaching of all pupils. But, as we will discuss below, musically talented pupils may require alternative or extended objectives to take specific account of their educational needs. Clearly focused learning objectives will allow for, and facilitate, the effective assessment for and of learning. This is an important theme that we will be returning to below.

In order to set challenging learning objectives effectively for musically talented pupils it is important to remember that they should be linked to carefully planned and appropriate teaching activities and learning outcomes. They should become an important structuring device both within individual lessons and across a scheme of work. For the purposes of this discussion the following definitions are used for these three important elements of planning:

- **Learning objective:** The main focus for the pupils' learning during the teaching activity; the main thing you want them to learn.

- **Teaching activity:** What pupils are going to do to learn your planned learning objective.

- **Learning outcome:** What you are going to see, hear or read as evidence that they have learnt what you intended in your learning objective.

There are some obvious choices that teachers have to make in order to plan in this way. They will have to prioritise what they consider to be the most important thing pupils should learn. They will have to be clear about how the teaching activity is going to promote this learning and how they will assess it (through the learning outcome). This is something that we will discuss further below. But if you examine a range of published materials it becomes apparent that things are not as simple as one might suppose. By way of example, listed opposite are some learning objectives taken from a published QCA scheme of work for Year 8 on the overture. As you read them, consider the following questions:

1. What would you consider to be effective learning objectives and outcomes?

2. What are the characteristics that make them effective?

3. Can you find any poor learning objectives and outcomes?

4. How could they be strengthened?

A common failing of these learning objectives is that they are either too vague or that they merely describe the activity that pupils will undertake during a lesson. Rather, they should describe the actual learning that pupils will undertake as a result of working through the planned activities. Surely 'pupils will learn how to compose in groups' needs to be refined and be given a much clearer and more focused edge? What are pupils going to learn about by working in groups that they could not learn through other ways of working? And 'pupils will learn about the role of introductions' seems similarly indistinct and descriptive. Perhaps it could have been changed to 'pupils will learn how to appraise the approaches that composers adopt to introduce musical ideas for different expressive effect in the openings of pieces of music'. These are not isolated examples. For further examples of good and bad learning objectives have a look at Appendix 4.1, which lists learning objectives from two other QCA schemes of work, one aimed at Year 7 and one at Year 9.

Setting well-focused and clear learning objectives is a vital part of planning for any teacher. What is especially important in relation to the teaching of musically talented pupils is that these learning objectives really do meet their needs at the correct level. This leads the discussion on to consider the role of learning outcomes which, following the definitions adopted above, should focus on the evidence that we can hear, see or read that indicate that learning has

Sample learning objectives from a QCA scheme of work for Year 8: The overture (exploring introductions and the development of themes)

Learning objectives Pupils will learn . . .	Activities	Learning outcomes
about the role of introductions.	Structured listening	Recognise the effect of the introduction.
about the significance of the introduction, the variety of messages it can convey, and the manner in which it 'sets the scene'.	Discussion Literary examples Composition on a literary stimulus Performing songs	Evaluate openings / introductions. Create an opening using words and sounds. Analyse how a performance begins. Understand information that is not explicitly stated and demands inferential reading.
to explore, recognise and understand how themes are used.	Listening and discussion	Analyse how music conveys character.
to identify how composers create transitions between themes.	Identify themes Compose themes	Identify and explore different ways to link themes.
how composers from different times and places use musical ideas in a similar way.	Comparison through listening	Identify and critically appraise how ideas can be used in a similar way by different composers.
how to compose in groups.	Composition and notation	Compare themes individually and develop transitions in a group composition.

© QCA 2005 (adapted from www.standards.dfes.gov.uk/schemes2/secondary_music/mus11)

successfully taken place. A common strategy adopted by teacher trainers when teaching new music teachers is to differentiate learning outcomes by using the all, most and some statements. A typical lesson plan document can be accessed on the accompanying CD. It contains space for the 'all pupils will', 'most pupils will' and 'some pupils will' statements that should indicate something about the expected outcomes from the lesson. One is not seeking to preclude imaginative or speculative outcomes in pupils' work through this system. Rather, one is thinking about what the most common outcomes could be for a particular musical activity and seeking to prioritise them at three basic levels. It is hoped that the work of musically talented pupils will always exhibit a high degree of creativity, albeit of a particular type (see Chapter 5 for a further discussion of creativity applied to the learning and teaching of these pupils). But these statements could be directly related to aspects of musically talented pupils' IEPs. An example of planning for differentiation through the all, most and some statements can be seen from the baseline assessment scheme of work for Year 7 (discussed in Chapter 3). Although these apply to a scheme of work rather than an individual lesson plan, the same principles apply:

At the end of this unit:

Level 3

ALL pupils will: create and perform descriptive music in terms of its mood/atmosphere; describe music in terms of its mood.

Level 4

MOST pupils will: create and perform music that reflects given intentions and uses notation as a support; maintain their own part with awareness of the whole ensemble; describe, compare and evaluate music created by the class using a musical vocabulary; refine and improve their work.

Level 5/6

SOME pupils will: take the lead in creating and performing and provide suggestions for others; use a variety of timbres in their work and make adjustments to achieve the intended effect; use sounds imaginatively and confidently.

Closely linked to the practice of differentiating learning outcomes for musically talented pupils is the practice of 'target-setting'. This means that specific goals or targets are set for individual pupils that are designed to raise their educational achievement. It will then be necessary to take action in order that these targets can be realised. The setting of a high standard of achievement for musically talented pupils is essential if their talents are going to be developed appropriately. We have already seen how targets have been set for Darren and Vicky at Kingsdown High School. But more generally, the teacher's role in setting targets for musically talented pupils will be an important part of their being able to:

- form an individual yearly action plan based on clear objectives

- identify individual pupils' strengths and weaknesses and plan work accordingly

- formally record pupil progress against National Curriculum criteria on a regular basis

- ensure a range of effective assessment and teaching methods are in place

- provide teaching which is explicit and selective about the areas of knowledge required

- ensure homework has a clearly defined educational purpose and that it focuses on appropriate tasks and especially the application of knowledge at the suitable level.

Target-setting should not be done by the teacher for the pupil. Rather, musically talented pupils should be consulted about the generation of particular targets and they should reflect their own concerns as well as the teacher's overview of their developmental needs. Remember that effective planning should have a practical and beneficial impact on one's active teaching role. Learning objectives should be shared with pupils and used to provide good structure to music lessons. If music teaching could be conceptualised as a type of 'performance', then individual lesson planning, learning objectives, the overall scheme of work, teaching activities and learning outcomes could be conceived of as elements of the 'score'. They provide something to follow but also something to interpret artistically. As we will see below, the interpretation may be as important, if not more so, than the written notes on the page. But the score needs to be there.

Designing appropriate teaching activities

The 'appropriateness' of a given teaching activity will change from place to place and over time. Individual teachers are in the best position to judge what constitutes an effective teaching activity for all the pupils in their schools. It is important that they are secure in their beliefs and not swayed by current fads or latest opinions. Professional judgements are vital here.

That said, there are some common elements to appropriate and successful teaching activities that should be noted. These apply to all pupils but there are some specific points of reference to the teaching of musically talented pupils that will also be identified.

Swanwick (1999: 45) develops an eloquent argument about the nature of musical expression and our roles as teachers in seeking to promote and develop our pupils' musical understanding. He describes three main principles that should characterise 'musical' music teaching. These three principles are:

1. care for music as discourse

2. care for the musical discourse of pupils

3. fluency first and last.

1. Care for music as discourse

The particular teaching method is nowhere near so important as our perception of what music is and what it does. Running alongside any system or way of working will be the ultimate question – is this really musical? Is there a feeling for expressive character and a sense of structure in what is done or said? To watch an effective music teacher at work is to observe this strong sense of musical intention linked to educational purposes: skills are used for musical ends, factual knowledge informs musical understanding. Music history and the sociology of music are seen as accessible only through the doors and windows of particular musical encounters. For it is only in these encounters that the possibilities exist to transform tones in tunes, tunes into forms and forms into significant life events.

(Swanwick 1999: 45)

Swanwick suggests that our care for music as discourse is a central component in the production of appropriate teaching activities. It is through carefully designed musical encounters that pupils have the opportunity to turn the raw elements of music into significant life events. There are many different musical discourses. As teachers it is part of our responsibility to develop an understanding of these various discourses and plan teaching activities appropriately. When teachers work within what might be called the 'traditional' field of music education, the path of musical discourse is relatively clearly laid out. Many teachers are secure in their knowledge and pedagogy when it comes to particular parts of the music curriculum such as Western art music, world and popular musical styles. However, this has not always been the case. Green (1988) describes a time when popular music had little standing or recognition within the formal music curriculum and the struggles that teachers had to face to broaden their knowledge in this important area. Similarly, her recent book (Green 2001) examines the pedagogy of popular musicians and challenges teachers to rethink their classroom pedagogy in light of her analysis. As an aside, perhaps the analysis offered by Green for popular music in the curriculum in 1988 and her careful consideration of the learning styles of popular musicians in 2001 have important similarities to the situation facing many music teachers in respect of the adoption of information and communication technologies in their teaching today?

2. Care for the musical discourse of pupils

> Discourse – musical conversation – by definition can never be a monologue. Each student brings a realm of musical understanding into our educational institutions. We do not introduce them to music, they are already well acquainted with it.

> (Swanwick 1999: 53)

Swanwick urges teachers to create and maintain opportunities within teaching activities for musical discourses between pupils and teacher. Most music teachers are aware that the majority of their pupils love music and the role it plays in their lives. Yet for some pupils, the formalisation of music within the curriculum is what squeezes the vibrancy and excitement from it. It becomes stale and monotonous, being totally divorced from their lived experience of music outside the school boundaries.

Acknowledging where pupils are at in relation to a particular part of their understanding is an important component of any effective music teaching. We could agree with Swanwick that pupils are already well acquainted with music, or a least a particular type of music. Bruner's notion of folk pedagogy reinforces this point and emphasises the importance of understanding the potential conflicts that can erupt within a learning environment such as a classroom if one is insensitive as a teacher to pupils' prior experiences:

> You had better take into account the folk theories that those engaged in teaching and learning already have. For any innovations that you, as a 'proper' pedagogical theorist, may wish to introduce will have to compete with, replace, or otherwise modify the folk theories that already guide both teachers and pupils.

> (Bruner 1996: 46)

3. *Fluency first and last*

Musical fluency takes precedence over musical literacy. It is precisely fluency, the aural ability to imagine music coupled with the skill of handling an instrument (or the voice), that characterizes jazz, Indian music, rock music, music for steel pans, a great deal of computer-assisted music and folk music anywhere in the world.

(Swanwick 1999: 56)

Swanwick's final characterisation of 'musical' music teaching leads into the often hotly contested area of musical literacy. For many teachers, musical literacy is seen as a kind of holy grail that needs to be upheld by every generation of pupils. Precisely what being musically literate means can be hotly debated, but at its crudest and most simplistic level is demonstrated by pupils being able to read notated music, usually in the Western classical traditional form of notes and staves.

Hence Swanwick's idea of musical fluency taking precedence over musical literacy, as defined in this traditional sense, is a useful transformation of this important concept. This is at the heart of what Swanwick is driving at in his definition of 'musical' music teaching. It reinforces what many of us know to be true from our observations of composers working across the country, e.g. Alex in his studio at the beginning of Chapter 3 or John with his guitar playing in Case Study 5 (also in Chapter 3). There is so much more to being a talented musician than being musically literate in the simplistic sense of being able to read the notes written on the score. Swanwick's focus on, and prescription of, fluency being a combination of imagination and skill is precisely right when it comes down to a consideration of musical practice in the classroom. Sometimes it is the musical imagination that fires a composer into action and leads them on a road of discovery through their instrument or studio equipment; in other situations it is their skilful instrumental ability of playing with pieces of software or hardware that inspires the imagination onwards through a composition process. Either way, imagination and skill are vital parts of musical fluency and are intricately related within the process of creation. It is these that we need to capture in the careful design of our teaching activities.

Pre-lesson rehearsals

Jo Salter was the first female jet pilot in Britain. Her account of learning to fly is fascinating reading and illustrates the variety of teaching and learning methods required to become a top pilot. Of particular interest was her account of how you can learn to fly without actually being airborne:

I used to walk around, rehearsing the checks, the switch positions, the radio calls – running circuits in my bedroom, plotting air defence tactics across a field, circling dogfights on bikes, even flying formation in my sleep. Rehearsal builds muscles in the brain and the brain remembers this much more effectively when flying and operating an aircraft. It is the beginning of an automated sequence where pilots react without thinking – essential for rapid decision-making at life-threatening moments.

(Salter 2005: 30)

And how did she begin to relate this process of learning to the challenges associated with learning to teach?

> As a teacher I employ the same lessons that I learnt as a student; I rehearse and visualise – how I am going to stand and how I am going to use my body language in order to convey my message. The spoken word is only part of how we teach. We have all experienced the flat teacher, the one who seems to no longer be there, whose energy has disappeared and whose presence is blurred. These are not the lessons you remember.

(Salter 2005: 30)

Pre-lesson rehearsals are a vital part of turning a lesson plan into a reality. Reading through, acting out or practising certain key parts of a lesson plan will be of benefit for all teachers as they seek to develop new strategies for catering for the needs of musically talented pupils. Structure explanatory dialogue or key questions and, if necessary, mentally script parts of the lesson plan ensuring that there is clarity and purpose in your words. Extension or enrichment activities for musically talented pupils should be particularly carefully considered and integrated into the overall objectives for the lesson.

During teaching

Having considered the main elements of planning for the needs of musically talented pupils, our discussion will now turn to factors that teachers will need to address during teaching. These will be considered under two main headings: artistry in teaching and assessment for learning.

Artistry in teaching

Teaching must be conceptualised as an artistic or musical performance. It is not an exact science. The music teacher's role is multi-faceted and complex. They can be an initiator, responder, facilitator, critical friend, listener, co-performer, improviser or composer and much more besides. It is vital that we do not lose sight of the need for skilful performances as being central to effective teaching.

Under this notion of artistry in teaching there are a number of important elements that the music teacher will have to include as they seek to address the particular needs of musically talented pupils. These build on common concerns in music teaching for any pupil but, as will be discussed below, they have a particular application or resonance for musically talented pupils.

1. The centrality of musical practice in the classroom

Firstly, the music classroom should be a place in which musical practice is the primary means of teaching and learning. This has implications for all pupils. Musically talented pupils need a rich and stimulating environment of music for sustained growth and development. It may be the case that the richer the environment then the greater the degree of growth for all pupils. The 'hot housing' of musical talent in specialist music schools may be the answer for some young people (more information about this is provided in Chapter 6). But for the vast majority of musically talented pupils our classrooms are where their talents have the greatest possibility of being nurtured. Carefully designed teaching activities that teach music through musical practice are the proven recipe for success.

2. The integration of curriculum elements in the classroom

Closely linked to the centrality of musical practices in the classroom is the need for these practices to be integrated within the key curriculum elements of musical performance, composition and listening/appraising. This is pertinent to the needs of musically talented pupils, who may have a particularly notable talent in one specific area. In these cases the requirement to carefully integrate and balance these elements is especially important. The model of music education at Key Stage 3 in the United Kingdom is clearly founded on this notion of integration. The National Curriculum document states that 'Teaching should ensure that listening, and applying knowledge and understanding are developed through the interrelated skills of performing, composing and appraising' (DfEE 1999: 20).

Similarly, integration of performance, composition and appraising underlie all the GCSE and AS/A2 level examination specifications. It could be argued that teaching at these levels should also exhibit a high degree of integration, with teachers seeking to harmonise approaches to teaching in areas of study or module studies.

3. The embodied musician as teacher in the classroom

Thirdly, and perhaps most importantly, artistry in teaching music demands that the teacher act as the embodied musician in the classroom. We can appreciate the importance of role models in the lives of young people throughout all walks of life. Good musical role models are vital in the development of musically talented pupils. As we will be discovering below in the concluding case study from Longdendale Community Language College, the role of a talent mentor was highly significant in the success of pupils studying for GCSE music. Not many schools will have the budget for such an initiative. But week in, week out music teachers are standing in front of their classes embodying – whether they like it or not – the role of musician as well as teacher in front of their pupils. It is crucial that we are seen to be a skilful performer, composer, improviser, critic and conscientious listener for our pupils, modelling good practice and, equally importantly, serving to demystify some of these things for our pupils.

4. Freedom and restraint: extension in depth and enrichment in breadth

Finally, the artistry of music teaching results in fine decisions being made by music teachers, e.g. when or when not to intervene in a pupil's creative work, how to question a pupil about their work in such a way that promotes a greater sense of musical understanding and engagement, etc. Teachers will need to make careful choices here in respect of their musically talented pupils. There will be a critical balance between freedom and restraint within teaching activities. Similarly, teachers will need to show careful judgement in extending activities through greater exploration of concepts, practices and ideas or enriching activities through broader study and application of ideas from wider contexts. Issues to do with moderating the level, complexity, pace and depth are complicated in these situations and require skilful handling at all times.

Assessment and the musically talented

The notion of assessment carries with it a number of issues, and these can be particularly pertinent when applied to the learning of musically talented pupils. There are many ways in which the term 'assessment' can be used in schools when talking about musically talented pupils. These include:

- assessment of nature of musical talent

- assessment of what to do about this

- assessment of the work undertaken by the musically talented

- diagnostic assessment

- assessment of what to do to help the musically talented take the next steps in their learning

- assessment of what materials are appropriate for the musically talented

- assessment to take account of pupils' interests and enthusiasms

- assessment of how the musically talented can be integrated within a class for regular units of work

- assessment on an ongoing basis to show progression

- assessment for a review of progress made

- assessment data made available for external moderation

- assessment for reporting to parents

- peer assessment

- ipsative and self-assessment

- assessment for the teacher to evaluate success of taught programme

- 'high-stakes' assessment, e.g. GCSE, A level.

All of these matter, and all have something to contribute to the teaching and learning process.

Here, we are going to focus on two immediate uses of assessment that impinge on daily practice. These uses are formative assessment, or assessment for learning

(AfL), and summative assessment, or assessment of learning (AoL). Assessment for learning is something that mainly takes place during teaching and will, therefore, be addressed in this section. AoL will be considered in the section 'After teaching', although we can all appreciate that the precise boundaries here are very flexible.

Assessment for learning has been addressed as a major feature of the Key Stage 3 strategy in the United Kingdom, following the work of Black and Wiliam (1998) and the Assessment Reform Group, and there are a number of materials for teachers to use in this area (DfES 2002; DfES 2004). Both teachers and learners are involved in AfL, and it is described as 'the process of seeking and interpreting evidence for use by learners and their teachers to decide where the learners are in their learning, where they need to go and how best to get there' (Assessment Reform Group 2002).

For the class teacher, using AfL principles in a class with a musically talented pupil should mean that they are doing very little beyond normal good practice. What will be different will be the responses that occur as a result of this. Let us begin by considering what happens when a new class arrives, or as a teacher takes on a new class or group of pupils. Baseline assessment often precedes a teaching programme. In some cases this can be conducted in collaboration with other schools within a local education authority (one example of such an initiative has been given in Chapter 3). With one or more musically talented pupils this process may yield little more than to confirm the existence of such pupils' talents. But what may be more helpful is for the teacher to build in baseline diagnostic assessment into the first few lessons of the teaching programme. Following this, and building on the information gained, the teacher is then in a position to build in AfL opportunities for subsequent activities and lessons. Here is a diagrammatic representation of this process.

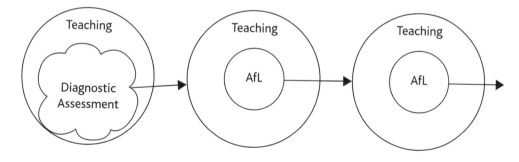

The teaching and assessment process

The process of baseline assessment here is used in a diagnostic sense. It is to determine the nature of what teaching and learning activities will follow, and builds into a developmental and progression-based course of study. The use of AfL techniques means that there is a dialogue between teacher and learner in order to work out the best way of proceeding. The techniques of AfL are likely to be familiar to most teachers, but let us examine them in the context of teaching musically talented pupils.

Key elements of AfL include:

- questioning

- feedback

- sharing criteria. (Black *et al.* 2003)

Music teachers generally seem to be in a good position to be using AfL techniques, sometimes without realising it (Fautley 2004). As an example, let us consider the case of a teacher working with a class of Key Stage 3 pupils on a group composition project. Whilst the groups are working the teacher will generally go from one to another offering advice and discussing ways the pupils can improve or develop their work. This will involve the teacher in making a series of AfL comments verbally – offering feedback – on how the pupils are working, and, importantly, on what they can do next. For musically talented pupils it is likely to be helpful for their development if they can be involved in the process, and if the teacher can explain why they are suggesting what to do next. It has been noticed that what tends to happen when teachers make AfL interventions in composing is that they tend to concentrate on organisational matters, rather than musical ones. In order to benefit the musically talented it would be helpful if teachers considered the nature of musicality which the interventions are supposed to help with. Or to put in another way, and as we have discussed above, 'to teach music musically' (Swanwick 1999).

So what is it that can be done? We know that teachers ask questions, and one way in which teachers offer feedback is the use of guided questioning to scaffold learning. Bloom's taxonomy of objectives in the cognitive domain (Bloom 1956) is a good place to start from when considering this. In Chapter 3 we considered applying elements of this taxonomy to help us understand the potential styles of learning that musically talented pupils might exhibit. In the figure below, Bloom's classifications are on the left, and the results from pupils are shown on the right. Between the two lies the area of 'appropriate questioning' for the teacher to use to elicit movement vertically upwards through the stages of Bloom's taxonomy, towards higher order thinking at the top.

Bloom		Music lesson (composing)
Evaluation		Make judgements about effectiveness
Synthesis		Use multiple understandings
Analysis		Reflect on understanding
Application		Use understanding
Comprehension		Demonstrate understanding
Knowledge		of; how to; what (etc.)

Bloom's taxonomy applied to composing

This upward movement can be achieved by careful questioning, and so it is appropriate for the teacher to prepare some potentially useful questions in advance. To do so, and to have a repertoire of questions that can be applied in many eventualities, it is logical to prepare question stems. Here are some exemplar questions stems that the teacher could use in the group composition exercise we are discussing:

Knowledge:	Describe ...
	Describe what you are doing ...
	Show me what you are doing ... (This is particularly appropriate with regard to 'teaching music musically', as some answers are contained in music by their very nature)
Comprehension:	What is the idea behind this?
	Can you show me an example where you ... ?
	What differences are there ... ?
	What is going on in your piece?
Application:	How will you go about ... ?
	What will you do to ... ?
	Can you think of (or show me) an instance where ... ?
Analysis:	How might it have been different if ... ?
	What happened in the middle section when you ... ?
	Can you explain what went on as you were playing that bit where ... ?
Synthesis:	What would happen if you were to put your ideas together with hers?
	What would happen if you changed that bit where ... ?
	How could you do this differently?
Evaluation:	What was successful in your piece?
	What changes might you make?
	How do you feel about ... ?
	Why do you think that ... ?

Using these stems when discussing work with pupils will enable questioning to help with understanding. The National Curriculum for England discusses 'knowledge, skills and understanding', and the objective of focused questioning is to help pupils gain understanding. A common occurrence after pupil composing activities is for teachers to jump straight to pseudo-evaluative questions, such as 'How could you make your piece better next time?', which presupposes the pupils are ready for this, having missed out the previous five levels of Bloom's taxonomy. Unsurprisingly, this will often elicit answers such as 'Not have to have Alan in our group', or 'Not use these instruments'. Instead, it is better to work up the taxonomy, arriving at higher order thinking sequentially. The musically talented pupil may appear to be able to jump straight to higher order thinking, but that does not mean they have missed out the intervening stages – it is more likely that they have subsumed them, and can move rapidly to the synthesis and evaluation stages.

So far in this section we have considered the role of questioning as a tool of AfL, and discussed how this might help musically talented pupils achieve higher order thinking. AfL also involves giving feedback to the pupil about what they are doing, and what they can do next. For the musically talented this is another area where it may be the case that the pupil appears able to short-circuit the process and arrive at understandings about these matters rapidly. Music is not a science, and so questioning and feedback cannot be based on a notion of arriving at 'the truth'. To respond to music proffered by pupils in a musical fashion means that teachers need to move to making responses in AfL exchanges that are not solely based on organisational matters. When our composing group produce their piece of music it is relatively straightforward to comment on whether they are playing in time or not, for our musically talented pupils we would hope to take them a stage or two further than this. Qualitative judgements are also important. This does not mean that the teacher needs to be apologetic for offering judgements of this nature. Far from it, the musically talented pupil will want judgements to be made in this fashion. As an example, let us consider the case of Brian, a musically talented pupil in year 10, and Carrie, who had 'music in her head'.

Case study 1 – Brian, the pianist–composer

Brian had been playing the piano since an early age. He came from an ordinary family, had shone at primary school and had carried on playing ever since. From the age of about 10 he had started to compose his own pieces for the piano. Upon reaching secondary school Brian had formed good relationships with the music department, and was often to be found there. During Key Stage 3 he had worked in groups at composing with others, but had also expressed a wish to work by himself on his own compositions. He used a keyboard and composed in a sort of shorthand that he then rewrote in immaculate manuscript. He showed his piano teacher his pieces and then started to share them with his class teacher. He was looking for real constructive criticism. He did not want adulation. He was genuinely concerned with improvement. His class teacher found time to discuss some of Brian's pieces with him, and began, as we noted above, by discussing form with him. Brian soon understood this, and after analysing some piano sonatas, was able to structure his ideas into standard Western classical tonal architecture. But Brian wanted more. He was concerned with the quality of his ideas. His music teacher was initially reluctant to go far beyond elements of form with him, but after some pressure from Brian, did venture into qualitative discussions. Brian's concern was that he wanted his compositions to have some meaning. This could be emotional or of feelings. Brian had decided that pictorialism could only go so far for him. Working with his teacher he composed pieces that were effective. Brian's teacher used structured questioning to get Brian to really think about what he wanted.

Case study 2 – Carrie, she had 'music in her head'

Carrie had played the flute and the piano from an early age. But during secondary school she realised that the flute was a 'common instrument', as she put it, so she took up the oboe instead. Carrie spoke of how she had 'music in her head' a lot. She would wake up to her own personal soundtrack, and these sounds would continue throughout the day, sometimes going into the background because of schoolwork, and sometimes coming to the fore. Carrie also sang in a local church choir, a group that performed standard Church of England liturgical repertoire on a weekly basis. Carrie began to listen closely to the 'music in her head', and used it as the basis for her composing. Her initial ventures involved word settings, poems were a favourite, and then settings which her church choir could sing of the Psalms. She said she composed knowing broad features of the music in advance; she worked out fine detail later. She enjoyed analysing music, and although she continued to compose, her enthusiasm shifted towards analysis and research. The teacher she worked with questioned her closely as to how she wanted her pieces to sound, and Carrie was enough of a technician to want her music to be correct in terms of formal harmony. She did not want to compose for feeling, like Brian, but for a considered effect, which her teacher helped her achieve by developing her understanding of harmony in context.

What these two case studies have in common is that the musically talented pupils involved knew, to differing degrees, what they wanted to achieve. The help they needed was with the execution of their ideas and AfL helped with this, as questions asked by the teacher steered the musically talented pupils into appropriate directions, and the use of appropriate feedback helped them achieve their goals. In the day-to-day teaching of musically talented pupils in generalist classrooms similar techniques can be applied. Sometimes teachers appear to ask 'guess what I'm thinking' type questions, whereas more valuable questions, possibly based on the stems outlined above, would be useful in eliciting detail and, importantly, in focusing pupils' thinking. The figure below shows the process of questioning and feedback represented diagrammatically.

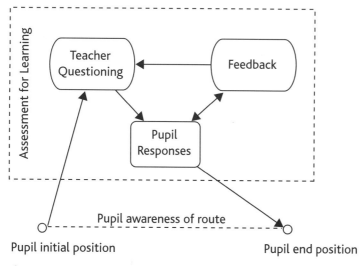

The Assessment for Learning process

In this figure the horizontal line along the bottom represents the pupil knowing that they wish to get to an end-point, but not being quite sure as to how to achieve this. The process of questioning and feedback that is undertaken as a dialogue is represented within the dotted box containing the AfL interactions at the top of the diagram. It is important to note that the musically talented pupil is a partner in this series of exchanges, they are not simply recipients of advice.

It is important to note that all of the AfL techniques we have discussed so far involve verbal exchanges and conversations, what might be termed 'professional dialogues'. Teachers often undervalue the role of these professional dialogues, and feel that they are not doing 'proper assessment' when they speak. In a report commissioned by the QCA in 2000 it was found that 'Teachers perceive the emphasis on summative assessment encourages them to focus on performance rather than formative assessment' (Neesom 2000: 4).

This report went on to say that this was particularly the case when being inspected:

> Some teachers perceive that Ofsted inspections create a climate of fear. They feel that they are expected to be doing something to satisfy Ofsted. They feel that there are 'mixed messages' about assessment and that there is more pressure on summative assessment than support for formative assessment.
>
> (Neesom 2000: 6)

In the case studies in this section the value of verbal comments has hopefully been made clear. However, many teachers will want to keep a note of formative assessments they have made during the course of a lesson. Many strategies have been adopted for this: some teachers use notebooks, others pro formas with spaces for verbal comments, some ask pupils to complete diaries which record discussions with teachers. Other teachers use electronic means, such as laptop or tablet computers to record brief notes, and some use purpose-made software packages. One teacher uses a shoebox for each class, and drops small notes made 'on the hoof' into it as she goes round the class discussing things, and collates these clippings at the end of each half term. Whatever method is adopted, recording of formative assessments should not be so intrusive as to prevent them occurring.

After teaching

The role of summative assessment (or assessment of learning)

So far we have considered AfL in some depth. The role of summative assessment is important and also needs consideration but not in the same depth. Summative assessment is usually perceived as being separated from a course of instruction (Shepard 2002), and can be considered as shown in the figure below.

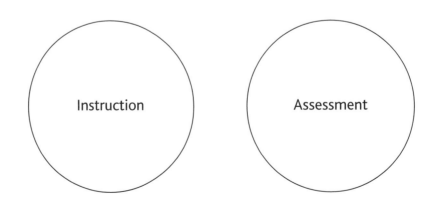

A traditional view of summative assessment

In the classroom, summative assessment will normally take place at the end of a course of instruction of some sort. Common examples to be found in the music context in schools are summative assessments that occur at the ends of:

- a unit of work: e.g. a test, a grade for performing a piece of music, a grade for a project

- a programme of study: e.g. an end of topic exam, an end-of-year exam, a grade for performance throughout a year, a term grade for achievement

- a key stage: teacher assessments and allocation of National Curriculum levels

- exam courses: e.g. GCSE, AS, A2 level examinations ('high-stakes' assessments)

- graded music exams: e.g. Associated Board practical or theory examinations

- competitions: local or national, after auditions or heats.

Most teachers will already be familiar with these from their normal day-to-day work. It is worthwhile to note that Black and Wiliam's research (1998) found that AfL has the potential for increasing a pupil's performance in high-stakes assessments too, so paying attention to formative assessment will pay off in summative terms too.

Many schools have excellent paperwork systems in place to capture some of the AoL data. Two schools, Tottington High School and Longdendale Community Language College, have made their assessment booklets available on the accompanying CD. The summative nature of the data being collected in this booklet is obvious. But pupils are also required to set their own targets and reflect on these between units of work as well as at the end of each year during Key Stage 3. The incorporation of simple evaluation questions such as 'What I enjoyed most', 'What I did best' and 'What I need to improve' at the end of each year is another notable feature that will encourage all pupils to keep track of their progress whilst allowing their teachers to formally note aspects of their musical development year on year alongside.

Ipsative and self-assessment

In ipsative assessment the performance of an individual is measured against how they performed in a similar task previously. Thus an athlete in training will want to shave seconds off their time for running the 100 metres. They are not comparing themselves with how fast others run the same distance, they are going for their personal best. Ipsative assessment also has a role to play in the education of musically talented pupils. In many areas of music there are opportunities for pupils to improve on previous achievement. In the case of the musically talented performer improvement can be a lifelong goal. In the short term, mastery of technical competences can be measured against previous achievement. For example, a pupil who plays the guitar spends time developing their dexterity at chord changes, a pianist practises scales getting faster and with greater fluency, a saxophone player tries to develop more complicated improvisations when playing with a jazz band. In composing, Brian, the case study pupil above, spent time increasing his mastery of the effective portrayal of feeling in music, acknowledging in which of his pieces he had been most successful.

Self-assessment can also be a useful strategy to encourage musically talented pupils and develop their abilities. This does not necessarily involve measuring against previous performance, but could be a way of considering how the individual had achieved in a task. Thus a musically talented pupil working at Key Stage 3 could reflect on the group composing project mentioned above and decide that they had contributed the majority of the ideas used in the group's composition, and that they had organised much of what went on, but that others had made important contributions too. This would be self-assessment, but not measured against previous performance.

The role of AfL and AoL in the teaching and learning of the musically gifted are vital strands of effective teaching. We have dwelt on the importance of AfL as a tool to be used during teaching for developing the competences of the individual, and of how it is important that AfL involves a professional dialogue between pupil and teacher. We have considered how AfL can also play a role in the improvement of high-stakes assessment, and of the role of ipsative and self-assessment in the development of an individual pupil's achievements.

Analysing teaching through classification and framing

Does what is going on in my classroom meet the needs of my musically talented pupils? This is the vital question that teachers need to ask themselves. Music education should meet the needs of all our pupils but, for reasons discussed in Chapter 1, the needs of gifted and talented pupils have often not been at the forefront of educational practice. So how should we analyse what is going on in our classrooms to judge whether or not it is really meeting the needs of our musically talented pupils?

> Music history and the sociology of music are seen as accessible only through the doors and windows of particular musical encounters. For it is only in these encounters that the possibilities exist to transform tones in tunes, tunes into forms and forms into significant life events.
>
> (Swanwick 1999: 45)

Swanwick's definition of musical encounter is a well-established concept. Its clearest definition is found in *Music, Mind and Education* (Swanwick 1988) where he contrasts the notions of musical instruction against musical encounter (pp. 120–38). Swanwick draws on the work of Bernstein (1971) to define instruction and encounter through the concept of framing and classification. Framing is '. . . to do with pedagogy, teaching style, with the degree of control that the teacher or student possesses over selection, organisation and pacing of what is to be learned' (Swanwick 1988: 121).

When musical instruction is characterised by strong framing the teacher maintains control over the ways in which pupils learn. Swanwick suggests that weak framing, where most of the control of learning lies with the pupil, can result in an increased possibility of musical encounter. Linked with the concept of framing is the idea of classification. Classification is '. . . to do with the exercise of selection over curriculum content, the way in which certain activities, perhaps "subjects" are marked out for inclusion in or exclusion from the curriculum' (Swanwick 1988: 121).

Strong classification is evidenced when teachers choose and fix rigid boundaries for what music might be studied in the classroom; weak classification gives power to pupils to decide the curriculum content.

Swanwick goes on to give a number of the permutations between the various combinations of strong and weak classification and framing. These can be documented on a simple graph, as shown below.

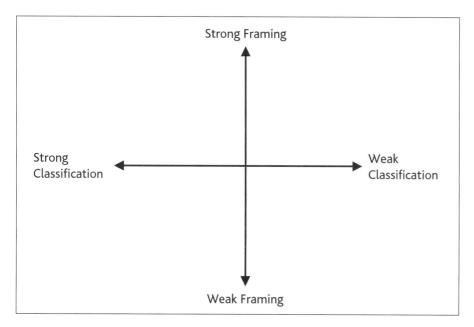

Framing and classification graph (after Swanwick 1988)

The use of this framework can be a useful tool to help teachers analyse their style of teaching. Firstly, some examples of this approach will be given from a number of curriculum projects that sought to introduce a range of new technologies to pupils at Key Stage 3.

Strong classification and framing

Within effective music teaching there will be a need for clear periods of instruction for musically talented pupils. In most cases this should be done speedily, allowing pupils the chance to then explore ideas, concepts and practices for themselves once general guidelines have been put in place. On one occasion within the *Reflecting Others* project (Savage and Challis 2002), an instructional phase related to the introduction of a piece of video editing software was allowed to continue for too long. Pupils were fascinated by the potential of the software and seemed keen and able to explore it for themselves. But their chance to move from a position of strong classification and strong framing (teacher-led presentation of specific features of the software) to any other position on the graph was limited and hence the enthusiasm of many talented pupils was frustrated for a while.

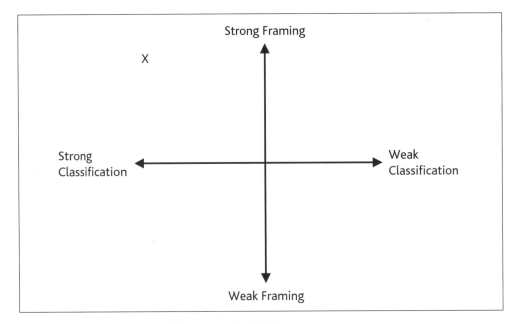

Strong classification and framing (after Swanwick 1988)

Moves towards weaker framing

In a previous project (Savage and Challis 2001), pupils were introduced to the workings of a basic sound processor. These sessions were conducted using a variety of approaches. By adopting a position of strong classification and framing, the teacher chose which features of the sound processor to introduce to the class, doing so in a presentational style that allowed pupils little chance to explore the processor's other features. However, after this short presentation pupils were allowed to take away a sound processor and microphone and, within a small-group context, explore both the demonstrated aspects of the sound processor and a range of other features that were easily discoverable. This was a move towards weaker framing and, although the classification level remained high, it did reduce slightly as pupils discovered new areas of knowledge for themselves.

Weak classification and framing

More significant moves between classification and framing occurred when pupils began to use ICT within compositional tasks. In the *Dunwich Revisited* project (Savage and Challis 2001) the use of support documentation played a crucial role. The *Dunwich Revisited* Project: Sound Generation Sheet (Appendix 4.2) is one example. Within this part of the project pupils had to use a range of

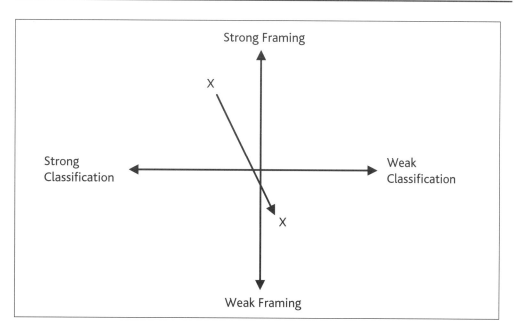

Move towards weaker framing (after Swanwick 1988)

ICT to help in the production of basic sound ideas. Although the task was clearly defined, the ways in which pupils worked, the resources they chose to use and, most importantly, decisions relating to the actual material of the musical composition (its selection, manipulation, sequencing and structuring) were within their control. An example of the resulting work can be seen in the planning that pupils did for their composition work (on the accompanying CD, where a recording of their final piece is also provided together with the original scheme of work). This represents a significant shift into areas of weak classification and framing, as can be seen below. Although the suggested way of working through the compositional process was clearly defined, there was flexibility within it to allow pupils to choose their musical ideas and develop their individual and group working practices.

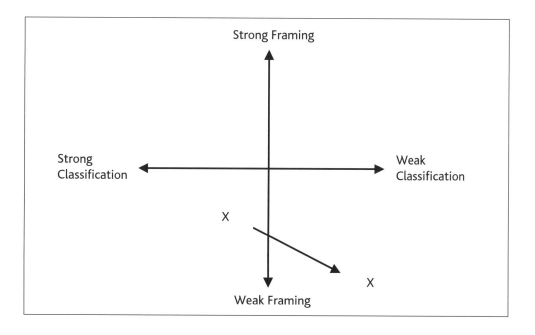

The concepts of classification and framing will be useful to teachers as they seek to analyse their teaching of musically talented pupils. It would be too prescriptive to say categorically which combination of classification and framing is right for this group of pupils as a whole. The point is that teachers will need to be analytical and reflective about their teaching as they seek to pinpoint which pupils respond well to certain teaching styles. But it is worthwhile bearing in mind Swanwick's observation, that weak framing may be the doorway to pupils encountering music in a special way.

Creating doorways to musical encounters

> Finding a 'doorway in' is an analogy designed to help teachers plan instruction to enable students to truly develop a structural understanding of music – an understanding that will empower their ability to listen to, perform and create music, and enrich their capacity to understand what the music expresses.
>
> (Wiggins 2001)

The metaphor of doorways is a helpful way to consider how one might increase the possibility of our pupils experiencing 'musical encounters'. The following section will focus on how these metaphors of musical encounter and doorways can be used to consider how the needs of musically talented pupils might be catered for effectively in the classroom context.

Allow for flexibility and movement between categories

Firstly, it is important to allow for and expect flexible movement between various classification and framing combinations during the course of individual lessons and throughout a scheme of work. Being too strong or weak in any one area for too long will lead to imbalances and pupil learning may be inhibited. The most successful lessons in music education are where moves between strong and weak classification and framing are effected smoothly and in a way that does not disrupt pupils' perceptions of the teaching style or approach that have been adopted.

All pupils are different

Secondly, it is important to be aware that individual pupils' experiences of pedagogical approaches will often be very different to what might have been expected or planned. For example, the supposed freedom of a weakly framed and classified composition task could be meant to be beneficial, liberating and a creative opportunity for some pupils. But for others the very freedom of the task might become the problem. The need for additional support or instruction (a move towards stronger framing but not classification) would be important to complete the task effectively.

Carefully worded learning objectives allow for musical encounters

Thirdly, musical encounters may be more common when teachers are confident to phrase learning objectives in such a way that allows for major shifts in classification and framing. Wiggins' work in this area is particularly fascinating. Her metaphor of a 'doorway in' to musical encounter captures the essence of this point. The teacher's role is to phrase particular learning objectives in such a way that the particular doorway will capture pupils' imaginations and cause them to pass through it into a realm of creative possibilities:

> It is an image to help teachers choose music from which to teach, and create lessons that will maximize student understanding of the music and of the ways in which music operates.

> (Wiggins 2003)

So at one level within this metaphor there is an element of strong classification. But the nature of the creative process allows them to make vital choices about the essence or materials of music:

> The very nature of creative process necessitates the manipulation of all the elements of music. Students cannot create a work without making decisions about virtually all of the elements.

> (Wiggins 2003)

Be open as to what counts as music

Wiggins' beliefs about the careful selection of musical content and diligent planning are central to effective music teaching. However, certain models of classification may need redefining as creatively exploring musical practices. For example, whilst it may be perfectly legitimate to use ICT to reinforce existing musical styles and practices, pupils may use it to produce music of an eclectic style, defined not by their teacher's pre-classification of musical content but by their own investigation, selection and manipulation of new sound sources. As far as is practically and theoretically possible, musically talented pupils should be given the opportunity to explore new musical landscapes throughout their music education.

This chapter has covered a lot of ground. It began with an overview of curriculum concepts and moved into a detailed study of the various phases involved in teaching music effectively. It has applied ideas to the teaching of musically talented pupils but also raised a number of general principles. It has looked at ways of analysing teaching, in terms of both content and teaching style, and has considered how the opportunities for pupils to engage in musical encounters might be facilitated in the classroom.

By briefly returning to our case study pupils discussed in Chapter 3 we can see a summary of mechanisms of the internal support given to them by their teachers in the table overleaf.

Case study pupils and internal support

Pupil	History	Identification	Internal support	
			Classroom-based	Extracurricular
Abigail	• Limited opportunities • Supportive family but no musical training • Not identified as G&T on entry	• Feel and maintain a steady pulse • Hear and repeat complex rhythms • Play in time with a backing track on a keyboard • Correct mistakes • Readjust timing • Sing in tune and maintain part singing confidently • 'Special' singing voice: clear, confident, distinctive tone • Compositional flair • Effective use of compositional devices (e.g. dynamic and tempo variations, expressive articulation) • Detailed observations in listening exercises • Able to express and justify musical opinions	• Solo singing opportunities in class • Extension work in class • Working within a talented group	• Free individual singing lessons with peripatetic vocal coach • Solo singing opportunities in school concerts • Junior and Senior Choir • Steel Band • Became lead singer in the soprano section • Technician support for ICT use
Emily	• SEN register for dyslexia and behavioural issues • Finalist in national talent competition • Lack of organisational skills • Lack of commitment to write things down • Unable to verbalise her thinking	• Compositional flair • Talented singer	• Challenging conventions with non-conventional composing techniques • Differentiated worksheets • Challenging tasks	• Singing lessons • Choir • Singing teacher developing her songwriting skills

Pupil				
Gemma	• Excellent singer	• Identified during rehearsals for school production in Year 10 • Excellent singing technique	• Melodic compositions using voice • Experimenting with keyboard accompaniments and chord progressions • Independent study for listening examination including preparation of revision materials	• Private singing lessons • GCSE study after school
Jonathan	• Previously identified as musically talented by staff at middle school • French horn and piano player	• Identified through collaboration with staff at middle school • Examination of composition work done at KS 2/3	• Arranging skills • Jazz harmony and modernist techniques • Adoption of more complex compositional ideas	• Accompanying role in school concerts • Performances at award ceremonies and open evenings
John	• Taught guitar by father	• Observation of guitar playing and singing	• New guitar techniques in composition work • Embellishing chords • Three-part vocal textures	• Guitar instruction • Forming rock bands • Performing in school concerts as soloist and in rock bands • Singing lessons • Tutor in school guitar club • Developing technician role
Stuart	• No previous musical experience or apparent interest	• Potential instrumental ability on the guitar spotted early during class sessions • Confidence and enthusiasm in performing for others	• Unusual composition techniques • Differentiated resources and materials	• Bass guitar lessons at school • Private lessons • School bass guitar teacher
Richard	• Leadership qualities • Strong vocal lead • Strong rhythmic ability		• Use of technology (Cubase SX) • Peer mentoring	• Choir • Guitar lessons • Performances in school concerts • Lead role in school musicals • School soul band

As expected, we can see different teachers meeting the needs of their musically talented pupils in many contrasting ways, both inside the classroom and through the provision of extracurricular activities. Many of these would fall within the categories of extension or enrichment activities, although there are some interesting developments in peer mentoring, pupils acting in teacher roles and pupils working within designated talented groups. Similar ideas will be discussed below in the concluding case study. We will be revisiting these pupils for a final time in Chapter 6 when we consider how their teachers made links with a range of wider musical opportunities outside the school boundaries.

To conclude this chapter we are going to return to some of the other case study materials that were collected for the preparation of this book. The following case study was one of the most interesting collected, primarily due to what may be the unique perspective of the writer who is currently both head of music and head of talent within her school. This case study grounds some of the ideas of this chapter in real practice and will raise a number of challenging questions. Before we move on to wider issues that affect how we support the learning of musically talented pupils in Chapter 5, her case study is a useful summary of ideas and issues that we have discussed related to the identification of musically talented pupils (Chapter 3) and how we seek to support their needs within the classroom.

Longdendale Community Language College is located on the eastern side of Manchester at the most northern point of High Peak, within Derbyshire but part of Tameside LEA. This college has over 900 pupils aged between 11 and 16 and is truly comprehensive, serving the full range of pupils' academic abilities. Judy Waters, the head of music and head of talent, wrote the case study. She writes with passion about the educational needs of musically talented pupils that have, she suggests, often gone unheard and unsupported.

Finally, staff from Longdendale Community Language College have provided an extensive amount of material drawn from their work with musically talented pupils. This supporting material has been provided on the accompanying CD and is a useful exemplification of the issues and strategies that are discussed below. As with all our case studies, the case study is preceded by a short statement from the school's most recent Ofsted report.

Concluding case study – provision for musically talented pupils

(Judy Waters, head of music and head of talent, Longdendale Community Language College)

The socio-economic circumstances of the pupils are broadly average. Around 16% of the pupils are eligible for free school meals, which is in line with the national average. Very few pupils are from minority ethnic backgrounds and none have English as an additional language. This is below average for schools nationally. The school is of average size with 926 pupils on roll, with even numbers of girls and boys. More pupils apply to join the school in Year 7 than can be admitted. Attainment on entry to the school is broadly average in relation to national standards. Results in the Key Stage 2 National Curriculum tests are higher than results in the other reliable tests that the school gives the pupils on entry. These suggest below average level of performance. Attainment on entry has risen in recent years. The attainment on entry of the pupils who completed their GCSE examinations in 1999 was below average, particularly their literacy skills.

There are 81 pupils on the special educational needs register in Years 7–11. 46 pupils are at Stages 3–5 of the Code of Practice and 19 are statemented. 9% of pupils are on the register, which is below the national average, and 2% are statemented, which is in line with the national average. The school's motto is 'we are all here to learn'. This accurately describes the ethos of the school. The aims of the school are focused on achievement and personal development. They are readily reflected in the work of the school. For many years the school has been setting targets for GCSE performance and is continuing to do so in line with government policy. The school's priority is to enable teachers to continue to improve the pupils' learning opportunities (Ofsted report, December 1999).

Longdendale was invited into the Tameside Excellence Cluster in 2000 and I was delighted to be trained as a gifted and talented coordinator in the same year, focusing on Key Stage 4. As I was employed as the head of music and, in a previous post, had led a successful expressive arts department, I was offered the chance of being made 'head of talent'. This was an unusual post as most gifted and talented coordinators had to focus on all aspects of gifted and talented in Key Stages 3 and 4. Coordinating the gifted and talented provision in a large high school is an enormous role and responsibility. It is essential that it receives the correct amount of time and resources from the senior management.

I received a great deal of training when the gifted and talented initiative first started. I soon discovered that the training was intense and demanded a significant amount of work and time. The residential work carried out at Oxford Brookes University and subsequent assignments and projects or reports could also count towards a master's degree.

Research has shown that thousands of highly intelligent pupils have been left to float through the education system without the correct tracking, support and guidance that will stimulate and stretch them towards appropriate levels of achievement. There have been many cases of pupils who are unmotivated and who find all the tasks so easy that school can become a drag to them. In the past, the education system was designed to focus on C/D borderline students. The special needs teachers were invaluable, giving extra support both in and out of the classroom but the 'brighter students' were not considered a priority. There have always been more intelligent children who raced through the work and ended up being given extension work that involved more questions of the same standard of work. How many times have teachers said, 'You've finished have you? Well just do the next two pages just to see if you really have understood it.'? This is one of the worst ways to reward our students who have worked hard to complete the given task. What often happens is that these more able students slow down their pace of work so that they do not get punished with more work as their reward of being 'first to finish'!

The profession is now far more aware of the benefits of differentiation. Differentiation is important so that we can cater for the individual and set appropriate work which will motivate and develop all pupils. But we have to give our pupils the opportunity to fail. Some musically talented pupils may go through their entire music education not knowing what it is like to fail. I have spoken to some gifted students who say they find school so boring. This is not arrogance, but a genuine problem and one that we all need to address as teachers. It can be a terrible problem for some children who may be prodigies and regress due to lack of stimulation and reward.

In a recent conversation with a gifted Year 10 student who was complaining about the geography coursework, I was shocked when she said, 'It's too easy! I will do it tonight. I can't believe how straightforward it is . . . there's nothing to it.' I quizzed her further and suggested she could look at it from a deeper perspective. Her reply was that that was true but because she would not be able to get any more marks, there would be no point doing additional work. This is a sobering thought! When pupils are used to being given A grades and now A*s we need to make working extra hard worth their while. The question of what these pupils could really achieve is mind-blowing. We only have a small percentage of gifted and talented people who really achieve what they are capable of. Many students just fade into the background and don't enjoy the limelight. Some bright students glide through the education process without ever being challenged. Some hate to be called a swot and are badly bullied because of their abilities. A small minority of students may burn out and regress.

I have seen a case in a primary school of a boy who could read fluently and understand all the maths tables at the age of 5. His first few weeks were terrible because he was forced to play with plasticine and work with his new book, 'This is a red hat, . . . This is a red door', etc. Parents were summoned because the boy had to fit in and show that he could cover the primary syllabus. Surely we have to have testing strategies that allow pupils to be given appropriate work straight away? The bright boy in question was so disinterested and frustrated at the work being given to him that he ran out of school, which could have ended in a tragedy. We have to empathise with what individuals are feeling. We do not have enough to stimulate the gifted and talented pupil – they need to have more celebration days and special rewards when we take time out to praise and acknowledge outstanding achievement. For a small percentage, the A* at GCSE level is a walk in the park. We may need to have an additional category that will ensure all students are delivering 'their best'. Why would you run a marathon when you could get the same medal for running up a flight of stairs?

I believe there may be many gifted and talented pupils who slip through the net and are not identified. This is especially the case in music. It can be a privilege of the middle classes to be given the opportunity to learn an instrument. Talented instrumentalists may have had lessons every week with their private tutor since an early age. If everyone had been given this opportunity then we would have to find more evidence as to who were musically talented and who were not.

A larger number of independent schools encourage their pupils to study one or two instruments and many church schools have a strong tradition in music, realising the benefits of music in the development of the whole person. Everyone who is a music educator is proactive about music being a wonderful way of developing the individual and releasing the true potential through this special sound art. We must, however, stop and question who really is a naturally talented musician. Every classroom may have pupils who have the capacity to become excellent musicians but who may not have been given the opportunity to show their talents.

We must be careful of judging our students purely on the Associated Board grades that they have reached, or even with just our own testing process. If true musical talent is to be shown then we need to generate the right conditions in our classrooms for this talent to be demonstrated. Our pupils need to be given a safe and happy environment. We need to encourage and ensure our students are relaxed. They need to be given time to grow and develop. I have seen pupils respond to all types of music in class and the most able musicians will be transfixed and naturally move to the music. Some pupils light up with delight. They seem to sparkle and respond so positively. The natural musician will receive a rush of adrenalin and the emotion will be shown in a physical way to the astute music teacher.

Pupils who are potentially musically talented but have not yet had their talents developed will love music. They will want to listen to all types and different styles of music. When questioned individually they may open up with enthusiasm and be full of questions. These pupils will desperately want to learn famous tunes and melodies. They will perfect their work and be quite determined and particular about generating a particular sound and will play naturally with fluency and feeling. These students will haunt the music room and will be desperate for any chance of joining in with musical activities. The naturally talented musician may never have taken a private lesson in their life but they will show incredible progress when they are given the opportunities to grow and improve.

Pupils who have been given private lessons, who want to practise without being forced and who find music a pleasure may also be naturally talented. These students will have a passion for their instrument and will want to study virtuoso performers. They will have times when they feel frustrated that they cannot obtain the sound they want to create. They will often place music before other activities.

Generally, the musically talented pupil will make amazing progress and he or she will often overtake music students who have been learning steadily for years. They will be like a sponge and thirst for information and will be intrigued by new styles. These pupils will often debate in class and voice their own opinion that will often be expressed passionately.

One of my pupils started to learn his instrument in Year 10. He succeeded in every music exam he took. The level of sensitivity in his playing and his thorough musical understanding in performance were apparent from the start. This pupil has sailed through GCSE and A level music without ever taking an Associated Board exam. He is currently studying for a BA Hons degree in music. He is called on to deputise in major shows and big events because he is a superb sight-reader and naturally intuitive to the requirements of musical directors. His many roles in music have given him a freedom and diversity to compose for England sports events, receive accolades from the government and co-write and produce his own musicals. Truly talented musicians are quite rare. They need to be nurtured and treasured accordingly.

Summary

- It is important to have a large vision for music education and what it can achieve for all pupils.

- The level, pace, complexity and depth of the curriculum should all be carefully considered as we plan for, engage in and reflect on our teaching of musically talented pupils.

- Assessment for learning is a particularly useful tool for helping support the learning of musically talented pupils.

- Swanwick's concepts of classification and framing provide a useful device to help teachers analyse their style of teaching and see if it meets the needs of their musically talented pupils.

- Try to build in opportunities for musical encounters for all pupils. It is through these that meaningful, lasting and significant learning will take place.

CHAPTER 5

Support for learning

- Creativity and the musically talented pupil
- Differences between teaching creativity, teaching for creativity, and creative learning
- Creativity applied to the construction of personal meanings through music
- Learning styles and musically talented pupils
- Application of multiple intelligences to musically talented pupils
- Illustrations of visual, auditory and kinaesthetic learning
- Learning strategies defined and distinguished from learning styles
- Musical talent and pupils with communication, learning, movement and behavioural difficulties
- The curriculum reconsidered for musically talented pupils

In the previous chapter we considered ways in which music teachers could meet the specific demands made by musically talented pupils within the classroom setting. This is a vital part of their role and of primary importance. Although these pupils' musical experiences may eventually become rich and varied, extending well beyond the physical limits of the music classroom, it is often from there that their regular, week-by-week musical development will take place. It is crucial that what goes on within weekly music lessons is well planned, practical and engaging for these pupils.

This chapter moves beyond the immediate classroom context to consider a range of ideas that should inform teachers' work in catering for the needs of musically talented pupils. Many of the ideas discussed below are becoming increasingly important in current discussions about the nature of music teaching and learning and have specific application to musically talented pupils. The three areas that we will be focusing on are:

- creativity and the musically talented pupil
- learning styles and musically talented pupils

- learning through performance: musical talent and pupils with communication, learning, movement and behavioural difficulties.

Creativity and the musically talented pupil

The notion of creativity in education seems to be ubiquitous and crops up in some surprising places. In music there is a unique and special role for creativity. We could expect that musically talented pupils will show signs of creativity in their work in some way. But before getting into too much detail, it is helpful to know what it is that we are discussing. What is creativity?

A good starting point for answering this question is the report published by the National Advisory Committee on Creative and Cultural Education (NACCCE) in 1999. This defines creativity as 'imaginative activity fashioned so as to produce outcomes that are both original and of value' (NACCCE 1999: 30).

This needs exploring further. When a musically talented pupil produces work how are we to know if it is original and valuable? To contextualise this within the classroom it is worthwhile to consider the difference between work which can be deemed to be original to the producer, and work which is original in wider terms. Boden (1990) considers that there is a difference between work that is original to the person producing it and work that is original to society as a whole. Boden draws a distinction between those acts of creativity that can be termed psychological, in the sense of having occurred to an individual, which she terms P-creative, and those that although coming into being in the same fashion, also have an historical import beyond that of the immediate. These she designates H-creative:

> If Mary Smith has an idea which she could not have had before, her idea is P-creative – no matter how many people have had the same idea already. The historical sense applies to ideas that are fundamentally novel with respect to the whole of human history. Mary Smith's surprising idea is H-creative if no one has ever had the idea before her.

> (Boden 1990: 32)

Each time a child plays a new arrangement of notes on their xylophone, or paints a picture of a hedgehog, they can be said to be being creative, not along the lines of a Beethoven symphony, or a Picasso picture, but in a smaller, more personal way. For the musically talented pupils in our classrooms P-creative work will probably be presented quite regularly. We can hope that maybe they will at some stage present H-creative work too.

For the teacher in the classroom three interlinked phrases relating to the teaching and learning of creativity occur. These are:

- teaching creatively

- teaching for creativity

- creative learning.

The NACCCE report (1999) discussed 'teaching creatively' and 'teaching for creativity'. The former is described as involving 'teachers using imaginative approaches to make learning more interesting, exciting and effective' (NACCCE 2000: 6), whilst teaching for creativity entails: '. . . teachers developing young people's own creative thinking or behaviour, and includes teaching creatively' (NACCCE 2000: 6).

Finally from the report, what should one aim for when teaching for creativity?

- autonomy on both sides: a feeling of ownership and control over the ideas that are being offered

- authenticity in initiatives and responses, deciding for oneself on the basis of one's own judgement

- openness to new and unusual ideas, and to a variety of methods and approaches

- respect for each other and for the ideas that emerge

- fulfilment: from each a feeling of anticipation, satisfaction, involvement and enjoyment of the creative relationship. (NACCCE 2000: 106)

Creative learning is less clearly defined (Jeffrey and Craft 2004), but teachers may meet it in the definition offered by Creative Partnerships: 'Creative learning . . . is a particular type of learning that occurs when a collaborative relationship between teachers and creative professionals is established' (Creative Partnerships 2005).

These terms can cause confusion for the teacher, a point recognised by Jeffrey and Craft: '. . . although the NACCCE distinction between teaching creatively and teaching for creativity has been useful as an analytical tool, it may, at the same time, have dichotomised an integrated practice' (Jeffrey and Craft 2004).

So, what does this tell us about creativity and the musically talented? We would expect our pupils to be creative in a number of ways, but the most apparent will be those musically talented pupils whose creativity is to be found in making music or creating music, in other words, as performers or composers, or maybe both.

Let us consider performing first. There have been many arguments as to whether famous individual musicians are creative or not. This depends, as we saw above, on what is meant by 'creative'. In the case of the musically talented, it seems logical to adopt Boden's description, and say that musically talented pupils who create new meanings for themselves are being creative. Here are two examples.

Case study 1 – Siegfried, a talented saxophonist

Siegfried plays the tenor sax, and plays it well. He enjoys jazz, and plays in a number of bands. His improvisation skills are developing and he has a good aural imagination that enables him to perform without having to work out too much detail in advance. As an improviser he is being creative, and is doing so within the context of the jazz numbers he performs. He says he doesn't know if he repeats himself in solos – sometimes he tries something new, other times he builds on what he has done before.

Siegfried's creativity comes from his performing. Improvisation, we can fairly safely assume, is a creative act, and Siegfried's mastery of his instrument allows him to improvise well. In performance it is his abilities as an instrumentalist that shine through. Improvisation can be seen as a fusion of technical competence and creative artistry, and in Siegfried's case we can see how he is a talented and creative performer.

However, it is not solely in improvisation that creative instrumental performances are to be found. Another pupil at the same school as Siegfried is Sara, a talented violinist.

Case study 2 – Sara, a violinist

Sara is a very able violinist. She has been playing from an early age, and her teacher describes her as a 'natural' violin player. Thoughts of school violins, and issues of 'in-tune-ness' vanish when Sara plays, and listeners tend to become caught up in the music. Sara enjoys chamber music and solo recitals, and performs with a maturity that seems beyond her years.

Sara's choice of music means that unlike Siegfried, she does not improvise. However, her performances are certainly powerful, and she can be thought of as a creative performer. Her creativity lies in performing the music of others in ways that bring meaning to listeners. As a young performer her teachers aid her interpretations, and so her creativity may be P-creativity, but others appreciate them too.

Turning to composing, we can readily see how the creation of a new piece of music can be thought of as being creative. However, what is it that distinguishes the 'haunted house' music of a Key Stage 2 class, from a famous recording of a masterwork? Again, Boden supplies the answer. The Key Stage 2 class are making music which is new to them, and so P-creative, even though the teacher will have heard similar pieces many times before.

Musically talented young composers often wish to compose using established forms, and often begin by emulating works they appreciate. Csikszentmihalyi (1996) discusses three aspects of creativity:

- the domain, which is the area of knowledge – in our case, music

- the field, which includes people he calls 'gatekeepers' of the domain – in our case music teachers, examiners, concert-goers, record-buyers

- the individual person, who uses ideas from the domain and has a new idea or sees a new pattern.

For our musically talented young composers, familiarity with the domain is being established, and they are trying out their 'voice' at making contributions to the domain, and are eliciting the assistance of 'gatekeepers', their music teachers, to help them with this.

Creativity is to be found in many guises. We need our musically talented pupils to master early creative utterances as performers and composers so they have the potential to develop. We will not want to deny them the opportunity of contributing to the domain, either now or in future, and so, in our role as gatekeepers, we will hopefully help them move on to the next stage in their development.

Learning styles and musically talented pupils

There are a number of different categorisations of learning styles. In this section we will look into some of the most common types, and discuss what the various classifications mean, and consider what the implications are for teachers and learners.

A lot of research has been done in recent years looking into the ways in which people learn, and much of this has been applied to learning in the classroom. For the teacher, it seems logical to start from the premise that a class of pupils is made up of a collection of individuals, and that these individuals all have different experiences, backgrounds, likes and tastes. Musically talented pupils who appear as part of a general class are likely to exhibit a broad range of learning styles, and so provision that is made for them does not need to be especially different from that made for other pupils. Indeed, it needs to be remembered that 'Research shows that the very able are not a homogeneous group, whether in terms of learning style, creativity, speed of development, personality or social behaviour' (Freeman 1998).

Where musically talented pupils are being taught in smaller groupings, then teaching in a variety of ways with awareness of differing learning styles is likely to help with developing understandings of new topics and concepts.

Multiple intelligences

In America, Howard Gardner (1983, 1999) proposed that we should not think of intelligence as being a single fixed component, as measured by traditional IQ tests, but that instead a number of different aspects contribute towards the intellectual makeup of an individual. Gardner's Multiple Intelligence (MI) theory suggests that there are nine separate 'intelligences', each of which exists separately, but which interlink one with another. These nine intelligences are:

1. **Visual–spatial intelligence.** This aspect of intelligence is concerned with the capacity to think in images and pictures, and to be able to internally visualise images.

2. **Verbal–linguistic intelligence.** People with a strength in this area tend to have well-developed verbal skills and be sensitive to the meanings of words.

3. **Bodily–kinaesthetic intelligence.** This aspect of intelligence relates to the ability to skilfully control one's body movements, and to be adept at the physical manipulation of objects

4. **Mathematical–logical intelligence.** Those who have strengths in this area tend to have the ability to discern numerical patterns and have the capacity to think conceptually and abstractly.

5. **Musical intelligence.** This is the aspect of intelligence that concerns us most. For MI purposes it can be described as having the ability to appreciate and work with rhythm, metre, pitch and timbre.

6. **Naturalist intelligence.** People with strength in this area are sensitive to the natural world and aware of plant and animal life. They may show an affinity to these.

7. **Interpersonal intelligence.** This refers to the capacity to be aware of, and respond appropriately to, the moods and feelings of others.

8. **Intrapersonal intelligence.** This describes the capacity to be self-aware and in tune with your own inner feelings, values, beliefs and thinking processes.

9. **Existential intelligence.** This refers to a person's sensitivity and capacity to tackle 'big' questions about human existence, such as 'Why are we here?' and 'What is the meaning of life?'

It is important to note that these intelligences do not exist in isolation from one another, but that everyone possesses all of them to differing degrees. If you think about your own preferences you probably know that you are better at some things than others, and that these areas are likely to correspond with different aspects of Gardner's categorisation. Let us consider two cases of school pupils that we may meet in the classroom.

Case study 3 – Adam, the keyboard and drum player

Adam is a 15-year-old boy whose skills at playing keyboards are remarkable. He comes from a family where his father plays in a rock band, but his mother describes herself as being 'not musical'. Adam was bought an electronic keyboard for Christmas at a young age and was soon playing music by ear accurately. He does not need to hear a piece many times before he is able to reproduce it. This is the one thing at which Adam excels. He finds schoolwork hard. At his primary school they were sensitive to this and encouraged his musical talents by furnishing him with opportunities to play in assemblies as well as giving him time in the day to play other instruments too. Possibly because of his father, Adam also showed an early interest in playing the drum kit and is able to play complicated rhythms accurately.

At secondary school Adam has been placed in low academic sets but flourishes musically. He gets into trouble occasionally but gets glowing reports from the music department! He plays drums in the school wind band and keyboards in his own band. He has been having drum lessons with a visiting music teacher from the County Music Service, who has been working with him on orchestral percussion, and trying to get him to read drum music, with, it must be reported, only a little success. Adam's 'ear' is so attuned that he can accurately reproduce complex rhythm patterns after only a few hearings. This gives him the appearance of reading the music – but he isn't. The same is true of his keyboard playing. Despite being technically proficient, he struggles with simple treble clef melodies, and again, relies on his aural memory.

It is undoubtedly the case that Adam, in MI terms, exhibits a high degree of musical intelligence.

Case study 4 – Lyndsey, the dancer

Lyndsey is a 14-year-old girl who has won a number of competitions and prizes for dancing. She has had lessons since she was very young, including ballet and tap, but she expresses a preference for modern dance styles. She also plays the clarinet, describing herself as being 'OK', but certainly 'not in the same league' as her dancing. She has a very keen sense of rhythm, which is evidenced in both her dancing and playing. She hopes to continue with dancing as a main part of her life after she leaves school, but feels she may not get much further with her clarinet playing, although she enjoys it.

Again in MI terms, Lyndsey exhibits a high degree of musical intelligence, coupled in her case with strength in bodily–kinaesthetic intelligence.

These two pupils are both musically talented, and alongside their clear strengths in musical intelligence also show intelligence in other areas. Lyndsey is a capable dancer, so her bodily–kinaesthetic intelligence can be considered a strength. In order to give meaning to their music, which needs to be understood by others, both these young people also need interpersonal skills. Adam, particularly, can be disruptive in some lessons when bored so he needs a focused programme that keeps him on track. Lyndsey does not feel she is 'academic', but knows she has to get certain grades in examinations in order for her to pursue her enthusiasm and talent for dance at a higher level. The implications of this are that education should not only 'play to the strengths' of talented individuals; it is important for the development of well-rounded people that a variety of their intelligences are catered for. This was something we noticed in the IEPs for Darren and Vicky in Chapter 2.

VAK learning preferences

VAK stands for 'Visual, Auditory and Kinaesthetic', and refers to the ways in which each of us prefers to learn, or to take in, information. The idea behind VAK is that each person has a different preference as to how they deal with information in the most appropriate and efficient way.

Visual learners

These learners prefer to read or look at pictures. They tend to memorise things by writing them down or drawing diagrams (e.g. spider diagrams or mind maps). They say that understanding occurs when things 'look right'.

Auditory learners

These learners prefer to hear things, to listen, or to be told how to do something. They tend to memorise things by repeating them to themselves. They say that understanding occurs when things 'sound right'.

Kinaesthetic learners

These learners prefer action and to try things out practically. They tend to memorise things by doing them repeatedly. They say that understanding occurs when things 'feel right'.

Many schools have developed techniques for identifying the VAK learning preferences of their pupils. Teachers have been encouraged to develop materials that address the same topic in different ways that can be appropriate for learners in all three styles.

Musically talented pupils are not automatically going to be auditory learners. There are many musicians who are technically proficient and expressive performers who rely heavily on printed music. Some professional musicians are so heavily reliant on music that they cannot perform a piece without it, even one they have played many times, e.g. the case of the cathedral chorister who is unable to sing the daily responses (a piece performed regularly and over many years) without a copy of the printed music. Other examples include pianists who perform a great variety of music, but all from print, and orchestral musicians who never have to play without music in front of them. All of these examples, and many more besides, would be classified under this system as visual learners. When visual learners need to memorise a piece of music to perform, they do so by visualising the score, or looking at the sequence of finger-movement they make on the instrument, and reproduce this in their performances. Some research says that visual learners look upwards when trying to access their memory.

Many published articles purporting to be based on VAK work state that auditory learners are 'good' at music. This may be the case, but it has to be remembered that VAK describes learning preferences, not absolute measures. A musically talented pupil could be an auditory learner, and the case study of Adam (case study 3) is an example of one such pupil. However, it is not the case that all musically talented pupils are auditory learners, or that all auditory learners should be encouraged to take up an instrument! Auditory learners who are musically talented are likely to find aspects of music which require the use of memory to be more straightforward than visual learners. For example, aural tests are not likely to prove problematic for these pupils, if they are sufficiently musically literate to reproduce in music-manuscript form what they have heard. Musicians such as Adam, working in non-classical traditions, are able to reproduce accurate performances of music they have heard directly. Indeed, many rock and jazz musicians do not need to access written music at all, and so their aural memory works well. Some research says that auditory learners tilt their heads when trying to access their memory.

Kinaesthetic learners who are musically talented are likely to reproduce performances based on hand or finger movements. There are cases of keyboard players who play through a piece on a table, reproducing the finger movements in order to reach the point they are trying to recall. For pupils such as these the learning is literally in the doing. Again, to say that a musically talented pupil who is a kinaesthetic learner should be encouraged to take up a movement-based performance, like Lyndsey in case study 4, also misses the point. This is a learning preference. It is how that pupil learns preferentially and it does not mean they learn only in this way.

Sometimes statistics are quoted which state that the population as whole consists of a majority of kinaesthetic learners, followed by visual learners, with auditory learners forming the smallest number. It is also stated that lower sets in schools often consist primarily of kinaesthetic learners. This may or may not be the case, but it seems logical to consider that not everyone does things the same way. Teachers too will have preferred learning styles. It is dangerous to assume that the teacher's preferred style will suit all their pupils. Indeed, the cry, 'I've taught it to them a thousand times, why haven't they learnt it?' demonstrates this point exactly. As mathematicians would say, 'teaching $\neq$ learning' – teaching does not equal learning! Teachers who only teach things in the way they would prefer to learn them themselves may be 'missing the target'. Knowing which learning style a musically talented pupil prefers may help the teacher present them with appropriate materials and strategies for learning. But they too will need extending, and if a lesson addresses the needs of all learners, whether V, A or K, then the musically talented will find something for themselves within that lesson too.

Learning strategies

Some theorists distinguish between learning styles, such as VAK described above, and learning strategies. A learning strategy is described as the means learners employ to deal with tasks and problems. Some psychologists argue that whilst learning styles are fairly fixed, learning strategies can vary, and can be both learned and developed over time. However, it is fair to say that there is some overlap between the two. The busy classroom teacher should consider them both as techniques that pupils employ to learn in different ways.

There are several ways of categorising learning strategies. This section will look at a number of the principal forms. These are Kolb's (1976, 1985) experiential learning cycle, Gregorc's (1979) four thinking styles, Honey and Mumford's (1986, 1992) learning styles inventory, and Riding and Rayner's (1998) work on cognitive styles.

Kolb's experiential learning strategy
Kolb suggested that learning involves transition around four stages of a cycle.

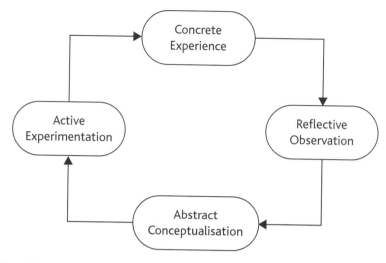

Kolb's experiential learning strategy

Simply put, this suggests that at the concrete experience stage learners undertake practical hands-on activities. These activities are then thought about in the next stage, that of reflective observation. This reflection then provides the learner with the means whereby they can make decisions, and in the active experimentation stage, learners can undertake problem solving activities using their newly acquired strategies.

In order to illustrate how this learning cycle could apply to musically talented pupils in a mainstream class, let us consider the case where a musically talented pupil picks up an acoustic guitar for the first time. This could be as part of a class performance unit where the teacher is tackling basic guitar skills with a Key Stage 3 class, leading to the performance of a simple melody. This begins with concrete experience, as the pupils are likely to already have some knowledge of how guitars are played, and begin by trying to imitate how they have seen guitarists perform. They will try to play different notes and will experiment with placing their fingers in the frets. Thinking about what is going on, i.e. undertaking reflective observation, makes them realise that they have to place their fingers quite accurately on the fingerboard in order to avoid a 'dead' sound. After a while, the pupils begin to think about how they have seen guitarists strumming chords and so they will think about how to place more than one finger on a string. This is abstract conceptualisation. From here they might try a number of strategies to reproduce this, maybe succeeding to some extent. This involves active experimentation. Realising they need help, the pupils consult the teacher, who provides them with a worksheet showing how to play the chords of E and A. The cycle begins again as the pupils undertake the concrete experience of trying to play the chords as shown on the worksheet.

Honey and Mumford's learning styles inventory

Honey and Mumford's work is derived from that of Kolb. Like Kolb, they say there is progression around a cycle during a learning experience. Unlike Kolb, however, Honey and Mumford say that individuals tend to have a preference for one of these stages. They categorise learning styles under four headings:

Activists, Reflectors, Theorists and Pragmatists. These can be mapped more or less directly onto the four stages of the Kolb cycle:

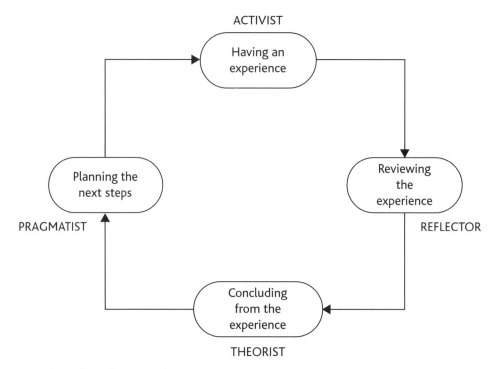

Honey and Mumford's learning styles inventory

The implications of this are that:

- activists prefer to 'get on with it'

- reflectors tend to take a step back and think about things

- theorists tend to analyse and synthesise data

- pragmatists search out new ideas to see if they can put them into practice.

Gregorc's four thinking styles

Gregorc's work is slightly different from that of Honey and Mumford and of Kolb. Gregorc suggests that there are different ways in which learners access and organise information. Again, these are described as preferences not fixed cognitive structures. Four such preferences are identified and described below:

1. Concrete sequential. Learners in this style are categorised as preferring to take in information in a concrete and sequential fashion. They are likely to learn sequentially, where things are broken down into a clear sequence.

2. Abstract sequential. These learners also prefer to learn in a linear and sequential fashion. However, these learners prefer to think in a non-physical way working with ideas rather than objects. These learners are likely to enjoy reading about things and forming theories based on what they have found out.

3. Concrete random. In this style of learning the preference is for using intuition to work with concrete experiences. This type of learner focuses on ways of working and on processes. They prefer to have a concrete outcome at the end of a learning experience but are happy dealing with open-ended tasks.

4. Abstract random. Learners who exhibit this preference tend to personalise learning. They learn holistically but filter this through how they feel about things. They are able to work well in group situations.

Cognitive styles

Riding and Rayner (1998) considered that learning styles, which they called cognitive styles, could be considered as falling within two dimensions. These two dimensions are wholist–analytic, depending on whether the person organises information as a whole, or in parts; and verbal–imagery, depending on whether information is represented using words or visual images. These two dimensions are seen as being independent of one another, but by considering them on a grid it can be seen how the joint influence of both will have an effect on how people act.

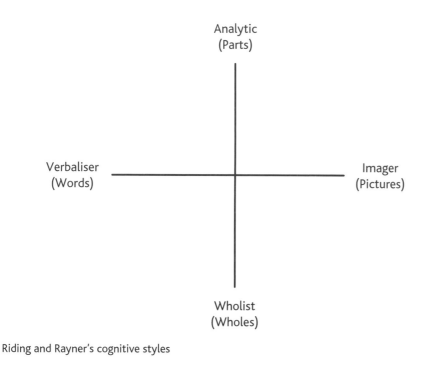

Riding and Rayner's cognitive styles

For musically talented pupils it is useful to consider the notion of imaging to include imaging in sound. Musically talented pupils may well hear inner soundscapes or, as Janet Mills puts it, may be 'Waking up in the mornings with sounds playing in their heads' (Mills 2005: 61). When inner sounds are externalised by these children, the organisation of a piece of music may well appear to arise as a whole. However, as we shall see, although these children are undertaking similar processes to other children what they have done is to have internalised the stages so fluently that they are rendered invisible.

Applying knowledge of learning styles to the classroom

There are batteries of tests available that allow schools to determine the learning styles and preferences of pupils. However, even without this information being available it is logical to assume that any given class will contain pupils who can be expected to exhibit preferences across a full range of learning styles and, as has been noted already, this is likely to apply to musically talented pupils too. In order to address the learning styles of musically talented pupils, it would be helpful for the teacher to consider how tasks can be addressed using a variety of approaches. This may mean that teachers need to think about how they themselves prefer to learn, as an obvious trap to fall into is that of always teaching to one's own preferred learning style. It is worthwhile for teachers to think about how the same topic could be taught and learned using a variety of approaches.

As an example of a project that can be undertaken by a whole class, let us think about a composing task and relate it to Kolb's work described above. This project is to compose a piece of music in response to a picture. The project is planned to allow pupils to compose using instruments and thereby work directly with sound. A project of this nature is functioning on a number of levels, not least of which being that it is a requirement of the National Curriculum for pupils to be taught how to compose. This composing task is suitable for a whole class to undertake in groups, but aspects of differentiation for and by the musically able will be described as appropriate. A diagrammatic representation of the composing task is shown below.

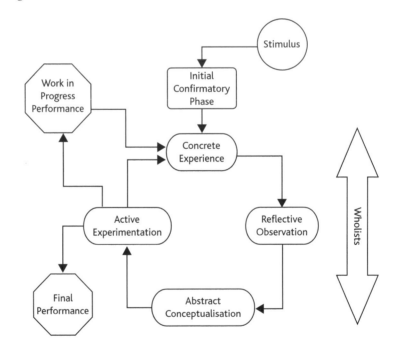

Compositional task flowchart

This figure shows the composing process beginning with a stimulus – in this case the stimulus is a visual one. As composing will be undertaken a number of times, it may be worthwhile experimenting with a variety of stimuli, using VAK as a starting point (although this is not the only way). Some possible alternative stimuli are shown on the next page.

Composing stimuli

Visual	Auditory	Kinaesthetic
A picture, e.g. a reproduction of a work of art	A piece of music	A repeating note pattern, e.g. on tuned percussion
Film extract, e.g. film trailer	A soundscape, e.g. city sounds	A movement to be depicted in music, e.g. an arabesque
Video extract, e.g. part of a TV programme	A poem	A gesture, e.g. staccato or legato (short, detached or smooth)
Advertisement, e.g. current advertisement recorded from TV	A short verbal phrase (as used by Philip Glass in *Different Trains*)	Rearranging sonic materials on a computer using a mouse (e.g. 'drag and drop' composing)
Photograph, e.g. perhaps taken by pupils	A descriptive passage, e.g. from a novel	Aleatoric or chance-based composing strategies, e.g. using dice to determine the order of events

It is important to note that VAK starting points are not addressing the learning styles of particular cohorts of pupils. What they are doing is providing a variety of starting points to enable learning and tasks to begin in a number of different ways.

Following presentation of a stimulus, the next stage in composing tends to be one where pupils discuss what they will be doing, and establish between themselves the way their composing will proceed. This stage is labelled the initial confirmatory phase.

Deconstruction of composing and wholists

Deconstructing composing in this way may seem unnecessary for musically talented pupils, but there are good reasons for thinking of it in this fashion. It is useful at this stage to remind ourselves that one of the things an understanding of learning styles tells us is that pupils learn in different ways. We are currently considering what is going on in a composing task when analysed in various stages. For some musically talented pupils this may feel like driving a sports car in first gear all the time. The vertical arrow on the right of the compositional task flowchart shows that wholists may well be able to conceive a piece of music in its entirety before they begin. According to Sternberg and Davidson (1986) one of the characteristics of gifted children is their ability to make rapid judgements about the wholeness of a task, then to decide what will be the most effective strategies for executing the task, and finally to monitor their performance in carrying out the task. However, being able to see a task in its entirety does not mean that pupils who are musically talented in this cannot improve. The notion of wholism does not mean that the music they produce springs fully formed from their imaginations. It means that they are able to undertake all of the stages with a degree of rapidity that non-musically-talented pupils will struggle to keep up with. To this end an understanding of what goes on in the process will help musically talented pupils too, and, to pursue the metaphor, will allow them to steer accurately, as well as change gear!

Returning now to the composing task, it can be seen that the next stages revolve around the Kolb cycle. Pupils experiment with instruments, generate sonic ideas, reflect and discuss what they have done, try some more ideas, and then add these to the overall group piece. At times in the cycle they will try to put all their ideas together in a work-in-progress performance. Following this they will undertake a period of revision, and work round the cycle again. In this sense what is going on can be viewed as spiral, as each visiting of the cycle takes place at a higher level than the one before; the pupils are not doing the same thing each time, but they are undertaking similar processes. Finally, at a point often decided by the teacher, there is a final performance of the piece. Often this will take place to the class, and the teacher will appraise what has taken place with the class.

For musically talented pupils, undertaking composing activities will allow them the opportunity to deconstruct the ways in which a piece of music is put together. It is important for them to understand that most music tends not be a continuous flow of new invention, nor a stream-of-consciousness outpouring of ideas. Instead, repeating sections are used and internal consistency is achieved by the use of musical architecture. As teachers we need to draw this to the attention of our pupils. After all, as Cook notes:

> . . . any music teacher is likely to have encountered the surprise expressed by untrained listeners when they discover how much repetition, and therefore how little distinct material, there is in a great deal of familiar music.

> (Cook 1990: 45)

Learning styles health warning

The sections above have presented arguments that pupils learn things in different ways. There are those who would argue that some of the theories presented here are not 'proven' scientifically. Some companies have made a lot of money out of selling courses built on applications of learning styles to classroom situations. However, what does seem important is for teachers to treat pupils as individuals, and labelling a musically talented pupil as a 'V' learner, or an 'abstract random', and then presenting everything to them in this fashion could be as dangerous as assuming all pupils are identical. What is most likely to be the case is that developing a series of different approaches or providing a varied learning diet, teaching topics from differing angles, will be beneficial to the pupils in many ways.

We have considered the type and nature of learning styles, and we have discussed how learning is different for individual pupils. We have also looked at the nature of learning preferences, where individuals demonstrate a way of taking in and dealing with information that is special for them. We have looked at a classroom composing task, and have considered how musically talented pupils would respond. We have discussed how a varied diet of ways of approaching learning tasks is going to be the most appropriate approach.

In the final part of this chapter, moving beyond the immediate classroom context to consider a range of ideas that should inform teachers' work in catering for the needs of musically talented pupils, we are going to look at how pupils with communication, learning, movement or behavioural difficulties may demonstrate musical talents.

Learning through performance: musical talent and pupils with communication, learning, movement and behavioural difficulties

Musical talent can be displayed in many ways and at many different levels. Amongst children and adults with these learning difficulties an array of musical talent can be found. The demonstration of this talent may be difficult for many of these children. Staff working with these pupils will need to consider the concept of hidden musical ability. This is musical ability that is often beyond a pupil's ability to demonstrate through speaking or writing. Much of their work is aimed at facilitating a demonstration of these hidden abilities through carefully designed musical performance activities.

Music Unlimited is a company in Greater Manchester that exists to challenge exclusion in music-making. Four full-time staff teach 35 sessions every week reaching over 400 people between the ages of 3 and 83 across Greater Manchester. They deliver a music curriculum for children with movement, learning and behavioural difficulties and since the mid-1990s have developed a scheme of work for enabling adults and children with learning difficulties to access music through performance. This is supported by certification at three progressive levels. Kenton Mann, the managing director of Music Unlimited, has written the case studies below on their work.

Music Unlimited's approach to the identification of musical ability

To access hidden ability we devised the scheme so that students would not be required to speak or write. It is all about hard practical skills and choices that may be demonstrated in live performance. We now use the scheme to offer incentive as well as reward. It is effective for children at P Level 4–6 and at Key Stage 4 and post-16 once the National Curriculum for music no longer applies. We introduced certification to credit people for the skills they already had and to make parents, carers and others aware of their often hidden ability.

The scheme is rigorous and demanding and is therefore always offered as a choice. Where a student cannot express a choice great care is taken to sound out advocates as to whether it is right to start work on a certificate. In such cases the delivery of the scheme may be structured to be less formal and less insistent over a period of weeks. Nevertheless, the criteria for success remain the same.

There are three performance skill levels:

Level 1: proving awareness

Here the emphasis is on finding out what people can do and working from strengths. Students have to show consistent involvement and ensemble awareness. Stopping at the right time ('Spotting the cadence' as we call it) without any prompt other than the music itself is a classic test of a person's musical awareness.

Level 2: ability to follow

Students are required to follow prescribed leads from the teacher. This can be very demanding for some. A student with cerebral palsy who passed Level 1 playing a pulse they found naturally may well struggle at first when asked to play a different pulse. Finding the right instrument for this is crucial. It is not expected that a student will be able to demonstrate their skill on any instrument. Many students find it impossible to produce a pulse on a tambourine but do so quite well using a stick on a suspended cymbal.

Level 3: ability to initiate

This is a difficult level as many people with learning difficulties have no experience to draw on in taking a positive lead. We have students who can follow and contribute to a performance at a professional level of understanding yet find it alien to actually start something. Those who pass Level 3 almost always become assistant leaders in practice if not in name.

Each level has five or six highly specific tasks that a student must complete in a live, albeit discrete, performance context. Tasks are not sequential. Most students work towards all objectives simultaneously. The following three case studies show how one task from each level is being dealt with.

Case study 5 – Rebecca

Rebecca is twelve. She is in a cohort group described as having profound and multiple learning difficulties. Music offers by far and away the best means by which she may make a contribution in school. She has just started Level 1 and she needs to be able to 'spot the cadence'. This means she has to play along with a short live performance then stop with the music without verbal or physical prompt.

I have explained to the classroom assistants that she has to do this without help. We do not use an assessment scale for our tasks. If there is any doubt we do not tick the box.

Rebecca loves playing keyboard so this is what we are going to use. She has a special chair so that we can get her close enough. She likes the sounds available and can reach out with both hands and press down independently.

Playing along is not a problem now so all our concentration can be on getting Rebecca to stop at the right place. The fact is that once at the keyboard Rebecca does not want to stop playing. This is not uncommon amongst our students who have a fine sense of occasion but massive movement and communication problems.

For the time being Rebecca is going to need lots of verbal and physical prompts to get her to lift her hands off the keyboard. When she learns to do it without help she will get her tick in the box. She will have made another step in her musical development.

Case study 6 – Shaun

Shaun attends one of our adult sessions. He completed Level 1 almost in one session and is hungry to succeed at Level 2. He has massive communication and movement difficulties but sophisticated intellectual control and awareness. Shaun can direct an improvised group performance with eye pointing whilst playing at the keyboard.

As part of his Level 2 Shaun was required to show knowledge of the correct names of five musical instruments regularly available to him. Shaun cannot speak. I state the name and he eye-points/nods to the corresponding instrument usually being played by someone else in the group. We agreed five instruments and I wrote five names down. A week later when I asked Shaun to nod/eye-point them out it became clear from the speed at which he pointed that he not only knew which was which but that he could remember the order that I had written them down in. I proved this by asking him to point out the last instrument in his list without actually naming it first. He was able to do this well.

Case study 7 – Stephen

Stephen has autistic spectrum disorder (ASD). Our development of the scheme for people with ASD is a priority for us. There are many problems. Stephen is an example of someone who has Level 3 technique but not that level of understanding.

We have worked with Stephen since Year 3 and he is now at secondary school. It was obvious from the outset that he had a flair for performance. He would sing Disney songs with the exact phrasing and inflection that he had heard on films and videos. One can argue about how a person is connecting with others through musical performance but breath control, range, diction and dynamic control are real. Not everyone with ASD can do this.

As one would expect, in his early days Stephen and his teachers found it very difficult to develop his musical talent. Stephen would become very anxious if asked to sing something he did not know. At other times he would sing desperately to connect with and please us and become almost a caricature.

To short-circuit the 'what do you know' trap we began to write songs especially for Stephen's group. We knew that children with ASD need visual clues to connect with what they are experiencing so we set the texts of Key Stage 1 and 2 big books. The effect on Stephen was dramatic. He stopped putting on an act and became absorbed in *Brown Bear, Train Ride, Can You Keep A Secret, Greedy Grey Octopus* and many more. He began to use everything he had learned for himself about phrasing and projection to sing along. He led the group naturally and at times quite beautifully.

At his secondary school in Year 7 Stephen is in a discrete ASD group but he is a valued member of the school choir. Membership of the choir has taken him to many places that he would not normally visit. Sometimes I see the disorientation in his eyes then the music starts and he knows how he connects. He has a wonderful music talent that we should treasure.

Epilogue

During our journey through Chapters 4 and 5 we have considered many ideas that relate to the effective teaching of musically talented pupils. These have focussed both within the classroom and outside by considering important ideas that should inform and facilitate our practice. Perhaps it is important in concluding these important chapters to return to one of the great thinkers about the nature and function of the arts curriculum, Elliott Eisner.

The curriculum is a 'mind-altering device' (Eisner 2002: 148) that is central to any educational enterprise. The curriculum, for Eisner, contains an array of activities that give a direction to and develop the cognitive capacities of pupils, by which he means their capacity to understanding, feel and act. There are a number of core influences on the curriculum that Eisner has identified and which can serve as useful concluding statements for us.

Teaching is an integral part of the curriculum

How one teaches something is constituent with *what* is taught. Method or approach infuses and modifies the content that is being provided. Thus, teaching becomes a part of curricular process, and curricular processes, including their content, become a part of teaching; you can't teach nothing to somebody.

(Eisner 2002: 150 [emphasis in original])

Within the arts, the act of teaching becomes an integral component of what is being taught. In the previous chapter we saw that framing is as important as classification in teaching music effectively to all pupils. The classification and framing graph may be a particularly useful tool to help teachers analyse their teaching style and content and map this against the needs of musically talented pupils. The teacher's active reflective role is crucial in ensuring that teaching plans, resources and activities are fine-tuned into learning opportunities and teaching activities that truly engage musically talented pupils. The generic recipes for music teaching that can be found within exemplar schemes of work, internet or published materials will deprofessionalise the role of the teacher, leading to prescriptive and bland formulae for teaching and learning that pupils will not respond to. They will certainly not fulfil the needs of our most talented pupils. The teacher is the performer and composer, the living embodiment of a musician for their pupils. For many pupils, their teacher may be the only 'live' musical performer or composer they see on a regular basis. This is a tremendous privilege and one that should not be surrendered lightly and sold out to formulaic curricula that do not take into account the particular needs of a group of pupils at that particular school and that particular time.

Pupils are an integral part of the curriculum

When students themselves are invited to have a hand in defining their own purposes and in framing their own curricular activities, uniformity is much less likely. The more teachers open the door to the suggestions of students, the more opportunities they provide for genuine individualisation.

(Eisner 2002: 152)

Secondly, Eisner reminds us that pupils are an integral part of the curriculum. A living and responsive model of the music curriculum will mean that it is not something that is 'done' to 'them'. They provide that 'dynamic context' within which curriculum planning and teaching become unified. Pupils bring with them a range of pre-existing musical qualities, attributes and experiences that need to be acknowledged and built upon. Giving a pupil an element of freedom in matters relating to the curriculum is not a new idea. As we have seen, Swanwick's discussion of classification and framing is one example of how teachers have sought to chart the flexible and skilful blend of approaches to curriculum content and pedagogical style.

Evaluation is an integral part of the curriculum

Evaluation occurs as teachers make judgements about the quality of the responses or the degree of activity and engagement students are displaying in the classroom. Teaching without evaluation would be a blind enterprise, almost as if someone were trying to teach a group that he or she could not see or hear.

(Eisner 2002: 150)

Eisner reinforces the teacher's role as a mediator of the curriculum by emphasising the important role of reflection and evaluation within teaching. Active reflection on teaching and learning is a vital part of initial teacher training and these practices should remain in place through our teaching careers. As performers and composers, music teachers appreciate the value of critical reflection on their own musical practice. Similarly, regular and systematic evaluation of our teaching is something that should inform our teaching of musically talented pupils. Often teacher and pupils make the best and most insightful responses when they are in the middle of something truly creative and exciting. This kind of formative 'evaluation in learning' is as useful as the more distant, reflective, summative 'evaluation of learning'.

Curriculum activities are an integral part of the curriculum

The curriculum activity shapes the sorts of thinking that children are to engage in. . . . How curriculum activities are designed, the modes of cognition that are evoked, the forms of representation that are presented or which students are given permission to use all affect what students are likely to think about.

(Eisner 2002: 151)

Finally, Eisner makes the familiar point that teaching activities are an integral part of curriculum planning and development. The choice and development of appropriate activities are at the heart of effective teaching. The skilful music teacher will produce a range of activities that allow all musically talented pupils the opportunity to experience, actively engage with both intellectually and aesthetically, and reflect upon the tremendous expressive power of music.

Summary

- Creativity will mainly be found in pupils making or creating music.

- P-creative and H-creative are useful terms in acknowledging the creative work of musically talented pupils.

- The context of the domain, field and individual are closely linked as we account for creative teaching and learning in music.

- An awareness of different learning styles will help musically talented pupils understand new topics and concepts.

- Visual, auditory and kinaesthetic learning styles are another useful device. Not all musically talented pupils will be auditory learners.

- Learning styles and learning strategies are both techniques that teachers and pupils can employ in different ways.

- Teachers should take account of their own learning style or strategy, avoid the temptation to remain with the familiar and be prepared to move effectively between styles and strategies as appropriate.

- Remember to treat all pupils as individual learners and do not force them in particular categories just for the sake of the theory.

- Musical talent can be found amongst an array of children and adults with learning difficulties.

- Performance skill levels are a useful breakdown of musical skills that give an indication of ability across a range of pupils with learning difficulties.

- The curriculum is a mind-altering device that teachers need to fashion with care to ensure that all pupils experience, learn and develop their musical skills and understanding.

CHAPTER 6

Beyond the classroom

- The role and function of music education networks
- Types of external support for musically talented pupils
- Some of the pitfalls of musical collaborations with external agencies
- Sources of support for teachers wanting to develop collaborations
- Funding opportunities for musically talented pupils
- Conclusion

Introduction

Music is not a single entity easily reduced to work in conventional classrooms but a multiplicity of activities, each requiring some specialist know-how, varying group size and different levels and types of equipment. How can one teacher and every single school provide access to such musical diversity as, for example, gamelan, steel pans, standard Western orchestral instruments in all their variety, a range of choral experiences, small groups playing rock and pop and possibly jazz, Indian music and the musics of Africa and the Pacific? Very rarely can students be said to be having a musically authentic experience. No wonder 'school music' appears to many young people as a sub-culture separated from music out there in the world, abstracted by the constraints of classroom and curriculum and subject to very curious arrangements for assessment. We have to do better than this. We should consider involving musicians of various kinds as part of a *music education network*, rather than see them as exotic novelties.

(Swanwick 1999: 100 [emphasis in original])

Swanwick's call is perhaps more relevant today in 2006 than it was when it was written in 1999. At the time of Swanwick's writing, there seemed to be a general acceptance that music education within schools was not what it ought to be. Many teachers and researchers considered there to be a widening gap between pupils' musical experiences outside school (in more informal contexts) and those within the school-based formal music curriculum. Current research at the time by the National Foundation for Educational Research highlighted the problem:

> Music, while benefiting from similar status to that of art, attracted the highest proportion of 'no impact' responses, registered a more limited range of outcomes compared with art and drama, had very low numbers enrolling for it at KS4 and, relative to other arts subjects, received lower levels of enjoyment in GCSE courses. Pupil enjoyment, relevance, skill development, creativity and expressive dimensions were often absent. Overall, music was the most problematic and vulnerable art form.
>
> (NfER 2000)

But many teachers found the above analysis to be overly bleak, based on limited research data and a dubious analysis. The current head of the National Association of Music Educators, Richard Hallam, wrote the following in an online response to the report on the Association's website:

> When I first saw the press release for this report my heart sank! The main finding about music seemed to be summed up in the quote . . . [as above]. Sadly my work as a music adviser, inspector and head of a music service had brought me into contact with classrooms where I knew this picture to have too much of a ring of truth for comfort. There are teachers out there, good, talented, committed, caring colleagues who nonetheless need to ask themselves some very searching questions about what and how they teach at key stage 3, about the numbers of students that they consider to be acceptable to study at GCSE and A level, about alternative courses that may be more appropriate for some of their students, about which of their students they are preparing and encouraging to go on to take up a career in music, including teaching.
>
> (Hallam 2000)

There is little doubt that music education has been transformed in the last five years. There have been many areas of innovation, not least the adoption and inclusion of a range of information and communication technologies in music classrooms that have changed the nature of music as a curriculum subject at a fundamental level. Similarly, a range of government-led initiatives such as the Key Stage 3 National Strategy have resulted in significant changes to our practices in assessment, target-setting and more general approaches to structuring teaching and learning. It is a sign of our professionalism that we should want to continually reflect on and evaluate our practice, making changes and improving our teaching in light of these new challenges.

Perhaps the next challenge for us as music educators is to respond to Swanwick's challenge and make those extended links with music educators outside the school boundary. This is not without its problems. Teachers will need to be careful to maintain quality and ensure a sustained programme of music provision across each key stage. So as we seek to provide, in Swanwick's term, an extended 'music education network' to meet the educational needs of all our pupils, and especially our musically talented ones, it will be vital to maintain a clear vision as to what we consider the ultimate purpose of music education is, why we consider it important for all pupils and how we should provide them with the best opportunities for learning.

This chapter will consider a number of approaches to the development of music education networks drawn from the work of different schools, starting with the case study pupils presented in Chapter 3 before moving onto two examples, one from a large and one from a small comprehensive school. These are provided to give teachers a range of 'types of collaboration' that may or may not be appropriate for their schools. Following this, a list of groups and organisations that give opportunities and funding for musically talented pupils is provided.

Case studies of external support

The table on the following pages provides a summary of information about each of our case study pupils discussed in Chapter 3. The final column indicates the nature of the external support that these pupils received. Often, this support relates to the pupils' participation in externally organised events such as music festivals, summer schools, LEA-organised orchestras or choirs, Associated Board examinations, or other workshops. These are well known as enrichment activities. In one example the head of music was allowed to use designated funding from the Gifted and Talented Excellence in Cities initiative to support a pupil's learning by providing funding for a musical instrument and to cover the cost of examination fees or subsidise the tickets to musical events.

St Michael's Church of England High School in Chorley provided a detailed list of extracurricular activities that help to further the musical education of pupils and especially the musically talented. While some of these extracurricular activities would be common in many schools, it will become clear that this school has extended and developed notions of cross-curricular, enriching musical activity to specifically cater for the needs of their musically talented pupils. The curriculum manager for the performing arts, and arts college coordinator, has written the case study on pages 126 and 127 describing the provision offered at this school.

Case study pupils and external support

Pupil	History	Identification	Internal support		External support
			Classroom-based	Extracurricular	
Abigail	• Limited opportunities • Supportive family but no musical training • Not identified as G&T on entry	• Feel and maintain a steady pulse • Hear and repeat complex rhythms • Play in time with a backing track on a keyboard • Correct mistakes • Readjust timing • Sing in tune and maintain part singing confidently • 'Special' singing voice: clear, confident, distinctive tone • Compositional flair • Effective use of compositional devices (e.g. dynamic and tempo variations, expressive articulation) • Detailed observations in listening exercises • Able to express and justify musical opinions	• Solo singing opportunities in class • Extension work in class • Working within a talented group	• Free individual singing lessons with peripatetic vocal coach • Solo singing opportunities in school concerts • Junior and Senior Choir • Steel Band • Became lead singer in the soprano section • Technician support for ICT use	• Participation in local music festivals • Summer school for choral singing in local music centre • Borough Youth Choir • Funding for keyboard, tickets and fees
Emily	• SEN register for dyslexia and behavioural issues • Finalist in national talent competition • Lack of organisational skills • Lack of commitment to write things down • Unable to verbalise her thinking	• Compositional flair • Talented singer	• Challenging conventions with non-conventional composing techniques • Differentiated worksheets • Challenging tasks	• Singing lessons • Choir • Singing teacher developing her songwriting skills	• Recent audition finalist in the X-Factor • Signed by music agent

Name					
Gemma	• Excellent singer	• Identified during rehearsals for school production in Year 10 • Excellent singing technique	• Melodic compositions using voice • Experimenting with keyboard accompaniments and chord progressions • Independent study for listening examination including preparation of revision materials	• Private singing lessons • GCSE study after school	• GCSE Bitesize and other websites for GCSE preparation
Jonathan	• Previously identified as musically talented by staff at middle school • French horn and piano player	• Identified through collaboration with staff at middle school • Examination of composition work done at KS2/3	• Arranging skills • Jazz harmony and modernist techniques • Adoption of more complex compositional ideas	• Accompanying role in school concerts • Performances at award ceremonies and open evenings	• Associated Board examinations
John	• Taught guitar by father	• Observation of guitar playing and singing	• New guitar techniques in composition work • Embellishing chords • Three-part vocal textures	• Guitar instruction • Forming rock bands • Performing in school concerts as soloist and in rock bands • Singing lessons • Tutor in school guitar club • Developing technician role	• County Pop Stars competition
Stuart	• No previous musical experience or apparent interest	• Potential instrumental ability on the guitar spotted early during class sessions • Confidence and enthusiasm in performing for others	• Unusual composition techniques • Differentiated resources and materials	• Bass guitar lessons at school • Private lessons • School bass guitar teacher	• Working with established bands in the local community
Richard	• Leadership qualities • Strong vocal lead • Strong rhythmic ability		• Use of technology (Cubase SX) • Peer mentoring	• Choir • Guitar lessons • Performances in school concerts • Lead role in school musicals • School soul band	• G&T workshop

Case study – St Michael's Church of England High School's approach to supporting the musically talented outside the classroom

St Michael's is a mixed Church of England comprehensive school. Its age range is 11 to 16, it presently has 1,047 pupils on roll and is over-subscribed. All but six of its pupils are white and there are no pupils on roll for whom English is an additional language. On entry to the school, an above average proportion of the pupils have already reached the expected levels of attainment for this age group in English, mathematics and science. The proportion of pupils with special educational needs is broadly in line with the national average for secondary schools. There are 43 pupils with statements of special educational needs. A majority of these pupils have a specific learning difficulty. Around one in ten of the pupils are eligible for free school meals, compared to a national average of around one in six (Ofsted report, January 2000).

There are a great number of extracurricular activities that help to further the musical education of the pupils and especially the musically 'talented'. The major development is the provision of a tutorial system – 'Glennie' – which contains those pupils across Years 9–11 who are willing to participate within whole-school worship and are dedicated to the cause of rehearsals. Admission is by audition and by letter to the head of music. This doubles up as the School Chapel Choir. This allows for further rehearsal time and creates a friendly atmosphere within the department across those musicians who are involved more than others.

A new initiative introduced from September 2004 was the smaller 'academy' groups. These are run by the students themselves with some teacher input. There are currently four groups – strings, woodwind, brass and jazz. Each one rehearses every week and performs in the major concerts through the year. This allows the more talented musicians to work at a much higher level, with open improvisation used in the jazz group, and harder classical pieces in the others. It also allows for the provision of solo opportunities wherever possible.

Other opportunities

- **Section leaders:** Appointed by the head of music, these are the musicians who show the greatest aptitude for commitment and desire to get involved. They also double up as the leaders/organisers of the academies.
- **Invitation ensembles:** These include the stage band and academies.
- **Individual music lessons:** These are provided for over 150 pupils and are organised in partnership with the Lancashire Music Service.
- **Theory classes:** These classes are run in support of those approaching ABRSM Grade 5 practical examinations or beyond.
- **Northern Chamber Orchestra within school:** The school has a partnership with the Northern Chamber Orchestra. Regular concerts are performed in the school by this acclaimed orchestra, including joint performances with the school choir and performances of pupils' compositions. They also provide workshop opportunities for GCSE pupils supporting the composition component of their work.
- **School productions:** Biennial major school productions involve over 200 pupils. More recent shows include *My Fair Lady*, *Barnum*, *Grease* and *Jesus Christ Superstar*.
- **Hungarian exchange:** The school is in partnership with the Kodály Music School in Budapest and organises a trip for pupils to visit the school every two years.

- **Opportunities in worship:** At this Christian school, worship is enhanced by music provided by soloists, small ensembles and two choral groups: the gospel choir and its junior counterpart the training choir.
- **World Arts Days:** There are two World Arts Days in Years 7, 8 and 9. For example, all Year 8 pupils have a day based on the theme of human rights. This supports the citizenship curriculum and, following an introduction with input from visiting experts, pupils spend the remainder of the day studying modules on art, music, dance and drama following related topics introduced through multicultural arts. Recently, Year 9 pupils experienced a World Arts Day directed by 'Bangdrum'. A workshop opened the day with an hour's presentation of different styles of world percussion and dance touching upon styles from Egypt and West Africa, among other places, with the overall emphasis on Brazilian street carnival styles.
- **Lancashire Music Service:** The Lancashire Music Service rehearses after school on Monday nights within the music department. They make use of the school premises to run county ensembles including the Lancashire Students Symphony Orchestra and Concert Band.
- **Other ensembles:** The following ensembles run during the week within the department: senior concert band, stage band, senior choir, training choir, chapel choir, string ensemble, steel pan ensemble, brass academy, string academy, woodwind academy and jazz academy.

To illustrate the work of this school, five recordings given by some of their musically talented pupils at a recent concert have been provided on the accompanying CD. They demonstrate some of the work of the newly formed academies and also GCSE coursework from both the performance and composition components.

The tremendous amount of work that goes on within a performing arts department such as that at St Michael's is possible because of a number of factors. There has to be a vision to establish such a music education network and this eventually comes down to strong leadership and effective teamwork between staff in the department. Staffing is obviously important too. This school has benefited from arts college funding for a number of years and this has had implications on the infrastructure of the school's facilities as well as what they can offer outside agencies by way of funding.

But it is hoped that smaller departments will take positive messages from the working practices of a larger department. By way of an example, here is an enrichment project that ran at a small village high school in rural Suffolk in a single-teacher music department. Although its focus was not primarily on musically talented pupils, it is a demonstration of what can be achieved when music teachers seek to work in collaboration with outside agencies.

Case study – the *Reflecting Others* project: one small department's collaboration with an external arts agency

Debenham High School is a mixed comprehensive school for pupils aged 11–16 years. It is situated in Debenham, a village in a rural part of Suffolk. The school draws pupils from an extensive geographical region. There are pupils from a wide range of social backgrounds, but the proportion from advantaged and supportive backgrounds is higher than average. The attainment of pupils on entry to the school is higher than average, but there is still a very wide spread of ability. There are 467 (217 boys, 250 girls) pupils on roll, much smaller than an average secondary school. There are very few pupils from ethnic minorities and no pupils speaking English as an additional language. The proportion of pupils (4.2 per cent) receiving free school meals is low when compared to the national average. About 8 per cent of the pupils have been placed on the special educational needs register, seven of them having statements for special educational needs. This is lower than average (Ofsted report, September 2001).

Reflecting Others was a collaborative digital arts project run between December 2000 and March 2001 by Aldeburgh Productions, Debenham Church of England Voluntary Controlled High School and Her Majesty's Prison (HMP) Hollesley Bay. Pupils and young offenders used a variety of digital technologies to collect sonic and visual material relating to the project's central themes of identity, community and environment. Having exchanged these digital 'scrapbooks' of material, each group used the material collected by the other group to make a series of music and video compositions that reflected their view of them. These were placed within a specially designed installation. A number of photographs of the installation can be found on the accompanying CD together with one piece of video produced by the pupils.

The *Reflecting Others* project demonstrated that a digital arts curriculum does promote and develop pupils' creativity. It was encouraging to note positive pupil reactions to their work, particularly their comments relating to the creative process and originality of the end product. Karen Dust, in an excellent review of the literature on creativity for the National Endowment for Science, Technology and the Arts, presents a number of other definitions of, and processes for, creativity. These are summarised under a general definition of creativity being 'a creative product produced by a creative person as a result of a creative purpose' (Dust 1999: 2). Quoting Howard Gardner, she discusses the idea of a 'crystallising experience' in the development of talent and ability. These experiences link people with the materials of a field in such a way that strengthens interest and increases understanding. Crystallising experiences can only occur, she suggests, if the right opportunities are presented (Dust 1999: 16).

In the context of our discussion of the importance of creating music education networks that spread across school boundaries and into the local community or wider into national networks, this concept of crystallising experiences is important. The experiences our pupils have of working with other musicians, playing in alternative musical venues, hearing their compositions played by other instrumentalists and many other examples of collaboration can all provide a highly motivating influence on our pupils and can spur them on to greater things. Perhaps those of us involved in music teaching today can all look back to inspirational teachers, remarkable performance opportunities or other enriching factors that confirmed and strengthened our desire to continue to work in music in our professional lives.

The *Reflecting Others* project placed the ideas and experiences of young people at the heart of a creative process. The final product of the project, the installation, was not just a reflection of their views of others, but also a reflection on themselves. Technologies became tools or vehicles for their imagination. As the pupils were employed in various creative tasks, their imaginations and experiences were stretched and challenged. The appropriate use of the technologies empowered the pupils with the skills needed to express and communicate feelings about themselves and others. As one Year 9 girl put it, 'There are many more ways of expressing yourself rather than just talking'. For some pupils this has led to a redefining of their own views about other people, both within and outside their normal range of experience. As teachers, we hoped that for some young people this had been a crystallising experience.

As a collaborative venture between a school, a local arts agency and a local prison, the *Reflecting Others* project was not without its problems. It is important to be honest about the limitations or difficulties of collaboration as this will undoubtedly be the experience of some teachers and departments in this new era of music education networks. So what were some of the things that were discovered as a result of working through the *Reflecting Others* project, which might inform other musical collaborative activities?

Acknowledge the range of experiences that all participants bring to a project

School-based collaborations do not happen in isolation. Project leaders, teachers, pupils and other arts professionals bring a range of knowledge and experience with them to any new venture. For pupils, their most influential musical experiences may have been contained or developed through the formal music curriculum. For a professional artist, musical skills and understanding may well have been developed through a deep understanding of their own artistic practice, possibly divorced from any in-depth consideration of how this might inform a pedagogical framework for others to learn by. When planning an external collaboration, it is vital to allow enough time for all participants to get together to discuss the venture and be open and honest about their preconceived ideas. This should include a representative from the pupil groups involved in the project.

Consider the role and influence of the National Curriculum or other examination specifications

All schools work within the 'confines' of the National Curriculum or other examination specifications. For many teachers, this has become a worrying straitjacket that engenders formulaic responses and diminishes the role of creativity in music education. From this perspective, it could be seen to legitimise certain activities and knowledge whilst outlawing or discriminating against others. But the *Reflecting Others* project proved that there are opportunities for innovative interpretations and practices for those who are prepared to take risks and work, as Kushner calls it, within the 'fringes of music education' (Kushner 1999). The National Curriculum is there to be applied and interpreted, pushed to the limits by those willing to rise to the challenge of incorporating truly collaborative, artistic practice in the classroom.

Develop cross-curricular approaches whenever possible

It is worth reading the National Curriculum online (www.nc.uk.net). Hyperlinks link cross-curricular themes extensively across the range of subjects. One might have thought that this meant that subjects are taught in a cross-curricular way, but this is seldom the case. Some of the richest arts projects that are run through collaborations between schools and other educational partners work across the arts or through links with other subject areas. The World Arts Days at St Michael's Church of England High School are one such example. Here, within the *Reflecting Others* project, music mixed in with digital photography, video editing and mixing, traditional elements of the visual arts, and classroom musical practices.

Problematise the professional artist's practice and process

Pupils are intrigued by professional artists; they are keen to explore elements of their artistic practice and the processes involved in creating new works. This can be a double-edged sword. One artist's individual, idiosyncratic way of working in a particular art form may not translate well into the classroom environment. The *Reflecting Others* project adopted a simple yet authentic compositional process drawn from observations of electroacoustic composers' studio work for pupils to adopt. This process provided a 'handle' for classroom work, yet reflected the world of the real composers' way of working. It was a key link to the successful production of material that was on time and of a good quality.

Place reflection and evaluation at the heart of any collaboration

Collaborations between schools and external agencies require time for reflection and evaluation. This is a vital strand of any successful project. In a simple sense, at the heart of the *Reflecting Others* project was a process of reflection on 'the other', and the expression of that reflection through sound and image. This motivated pupils. Their sense of personal identity and community was very strong. But it is important that leaders of collaborative projects allow that space for considered reflection on the collaboration itself. 'Reflection in action' and 'Reflection on action' have important parallels with their assessment-based counterparts, AfL and AoL. Both should become a natural part of our working process as we seek to collaborate with other agencies.

Summary

The *Reflecting Others* project taught all those involved to take risks in their collaborations. When seeking to work collaboratively there is little point in settling for the normal and everyday – after all, that is what can be done through regular teaching opportunities. Going for the extraordinary and allowing opportunities for truly creative tasks, rather than the re-creative, will captivate and motivate pupils, as will seeking to design new schemes of work that encourage creativity, allow for personal responses and build on adaptations of authentic compositional practices and procedures. Finally, *Reflecting Others* taught us to allow time for self-reflection and self-evaluation and to let pupils' work stand for what it is. It has tremendous value. The best of it can stand alongside the work of professional artists without embarrassment.

Information about sources of support

There are many sources of support for music teachers looking to work collaboratively and provide a greater range of opportunities for their musically talented pupils. A number of these will be regional and similar to those identified in the case studies above (e.g. local education authorities, regional arts agencies, private sponsors, etc.). What follows are some useful national contacts and sources of further information for schools seeking to develop this important aspect of their work and perhaps explore funding opportunities. There are also links to specific organisations or groups that will support the performance and composition work of musically talented pupils. The short piece of text following each organisation's heading and address has been adapted from the homepages of their respective websites and gives a brief flavour of the work that they do.

General sources of support

Creative Generation

(www.creativegeneration.org.uk)

Creative Generation exists to connect gifted and talented young artists with their future. In the teacher's area there is an opportunity to access the latest pedagogical guidance and share experiences. There is also a searchable database of providers of specialist arts opportunities.

Federation of Music Services

(www.federationmusic.org.uk)

The Federation of Music Services has become widely recognised as a highly focused voice for music services. They have a positive working relationship with the DfES, Ofsted and the QCA as well as fellow music organisations such as MEC and NAME.

Associated Board of the Royal Schools of Music

(www.abrsm.ac.uk)

The Associated Board of the Royal Schools of Music is the world's leading music examining board. Over 620,000 candidates take their music exams each year in more than 90 countries around the world. They also run professional development courses for teachers, and ABRSM Publishing publishes a wide range of repertoire, music books and CDs.

Musical Futures

(www.musicalfutures.org.uk)

Musical Futures is a project funded by the Paul Hamlyn Foundation. It has been set up to facilitate learning about, creating and sharing music. Although it is centred on three main geographical areas (Leeds, Herefordshire and Nottingham), through their website teachers and pupils can ask questions, publish their work and share ideas with other students, teachers and musicians.

Youth Music

(www.youthmusic.org.uk)

Youth Music is a UK-wide charity set up in 1999 to provide high-quality and diverse music-making opportunities for 0- to 18-year-olds. It targets young people living in areas of social and economic need who might otherwise lack musical opportunities. It predominantly supports activities that are held outside school hours.

Music Education Council

(www.mec.org.uk)

The Music Education Council – the umbrella body for all organisations connected with music education in the United Kingdom – exists to bring together and provide a forum for those organisations to debate issues affecting music education and to make representation and promote appropriate action at local, national and international level.

Music for Youth

(www.mfy.org.uk)

Music for Youth is an educational charity with a worldwide reputation for its work in music education. It provides free access to educational and performance opportunities for all kinds of groups of young musicians and audiences through a nationwide series of festivals and concerts.

National Federation of Music Societies

(www.nfms.org.uk)

The National Federation of Music Societies represents and supports amateur and semi-professional music groups of all genres throughout the United Kingdom. It provides a comprehensive range of artistic and administrative services and development and training opportunities. With over 2,000 member societies, it represents over 138,000 musicians and music lovers throughout the UK.

National Association of Music Educators (NAME)

(www.name2.org.uk)

The National Association of Music Educators exists to support its members in the development of music education of the highest quality that is accessible to all. They seek to achieve this by contributing to the creation of a strong and unified voice for music education nationally, providing a forum for professional exchange and collaboration with other appropriate organisations.

Jazz Services

(www.jazzservices.org.uk)

Jazz Services runs the most comprehensive database on the UK jazz scene – a wealth of information gathered over years of supporting and encouraging British musicians. It exists to promote and support the development of jazz in the UK. It offers services in information, education, touring support, communications, marketing and publishing.

National Association for Able Children in Education (NACE)

(www.nace.co.uk)

NACE exists solely to support the daily work of teachers providing for pupils with high abilities whilst enabling all pupils to flourish. The Association is a charity, established in 1984 by members of the Schools Council Gifted Child Project, to bring together and support all those with an interest in the education of able, gifted and talented children.

Its members are teachers, head teachers, advisers, inspectors, psychologists, researchers, writers, independent consultants, student teachers and parents. They include people who are new to teaching able pupils and the leading national and international practitioners in the field – a wealth of experience used to benefit teachers and their pupils.

National Academy for Gifted and Talented Youth

(www.nagty.ac.uk)

The government established the National Academy for Gifted and Talented Youth (NAGTY) in 2002. Its role is to drive forward improvements in gifted and talented education by developing a national catalyst that can provide leadership and support for professionals working in this field. To achieve this NAGTY works with students, parents, teachers, education professionals, specialist providers, universities and business.

Schools Music Association

(www.schoolsmusic.org.uk)

The Schools Music Association is recognised as a national voice for music in education. It provides an essential network for music teachers that serves as a vital link between those working with young people and the policy makers at local, regional and national level. Officers from the SMA meet regularly with representatives from the QCA, DfES, GTC, TTA, DCMS and other statutory bodies to reinforce the place of music in education.

National Early Music Association

(www.nema-uk.org)

The National Early Music Association of the UK has existed since 1981 to bring together all concerned with early music and to forge links with other early music organisations in the UK and around the world. For a small annual fee, members of NEMA receive the annual Early Music Yearbook, an invaluable handbook containing details of professional and amateur enthusiasts worldwide as well as of societies, magazines, instrument makers and much more. There is an extensive network of amateur musicians accessible through the regional forums, which organise regular workshops and music days at which young musicians are always welcome.

Funding opportunities for musically talented pupils and their teachers

Awards for Young Musicians (AYM)

(www.a-y-m.org.uk)

AYM is a registered charity established in 1998. It assists musically gifted children (aged 5–18), by giving them financial awards to help them achieve their potential.

DfES Music and Dance Scheme

(www.dfes.gov.uk/mds)

If a child has a special talent in music or dance, would benefit from special training, and requires help with the costs of their training then the Department for Education and Skill's Music and Dance scheme could help. They currently enable over 800 exceptionally talented children to have access to the best specialist music and dance training available alongside a good academic education. The Department is also piloting a new national grants scheme for similar children to access locally high-quality, out-of-school-hours training. Their website gives information about the music and dance scheme, which schools and centres participate in it, how one can apply for a place, and about other new and future developments.

Hattori Foundation

(www.hattorifoundation.org.uk)

The Hattori Foundation was established as an educational trust by the Hattori family and granted charity status in 1992. The aim of the Foundation in the field of music is to encourage and assist exceptionally talented young instrumental soloists or chamber ensembles who are British nationals or resident in the UK and whose talent and achievements give promise of an international career.

Creative Partnerships

(www.creative-partnerships.com)

Creative Partnerships provides school children across England with the opportunity to develop creativity in learning and to take part in cultural activities of the highest quality. It is not a funding body but aims to establish genuine collaborative partnerships to enable the development of projects that reflect the interests, specialisms and shared vision of those involved. Based at Arts Council England, Creative Partnerships has a unique approach to working with schools. Firstly, it helps schools to identify their individual needs and then, secondly, it enables them to develop long-term, sustainable partnerships with organisations and individuals including architects, theatre companies, museums, cinemas, historic buildings, dance studios, recording studios, orchestras, film-makers, website designers and many others.

Felicity Belfield Music Trust

(Blanda House, Chaffcombe, Chard, Somerset, TA20 4BL)

This Trust was formed in 1990 to enable students to have an instrument worthy of their talents, which they would otherwise be unable to afford. Students can apply at any age up to 20. Instruments are loaned to students until they are 25 when the instrument must be returned or purchased from the Trust. Students should be able to prove exceptional talent and financial need. A reference is required from the applicant's music teacher.

Benslow Musical Instrument Loan Scheme

(www.benslow.org)

The Scheme lends quality instruments – mostly strings, with some woodwind – to promising young players and students who could not otherwise afford the calibre of instrument they need. Applications are invited from young musicians of any age, from primary school to advanced study. Borrowers are selected on the basis of musical promise and financial need. In most cases, instruments are lent for an initial period of three years or until the end of a recognised course of study. All instruments are insured by the Scheme.

EMI Music Sound Foundation

(www.emimusicsoundfoundation.com)

The Foundation was established by EMI in 1997 to commemorate the centenary of EMI Records. It is an independent charity that is dedicated to the improvement of music education. Applications are accepted in March and September from: non-specialist schools to fund music education; individual music students in full-time education to fund instrument purchase; music teachers to fund training. The Foundation also funds bursaries for music students through selected colleges and is a major sponsor of performing arts colleges as part of the government's specialist schools scheme, having successfully sponsored 25 schools to date.

Musicians Benevolent Fund Awards for Under-18s

(www.mbf.org.uk)

Awards of up to £1,000 are made to outstandingly talented instrumentalists of school age. Awards are offered towards the costs of instrument purchase, private music lessons, or fees and occasionally travel expenses to the junior departments of the principal music colleges in the UK. Awards are made annually.

John Fletcher Trust Fund

(e-mail: thejohnfletchertrustfund@hotmail.com)

The Fund is open to talented young brass players of pre-college age (usually between 12 and 18 years). Its purpose is to advance the musical education and orchestral playing of talented young brass players who are not already full-time music students at a recognised college of music. Bursaries are mainly given to brass players attending the courses run by the National Youth Orchestra, the National Youth Wind Orchestra, the National Youth Brass Band and the Northern Junior Philharmonic Orchestra.

Musicians Benevolent Fund: Awards, Scholarships and Competitions for Young Musicians

(www.mbf.org.uk/ngen_public/index.asp)

There are a large number of resources available to students, parents and teachers to assist with the funding of study projects for gifted musicians, and the MBF database and Awards Wizard can help you to identify many of the music awards and scholarships that are available. Their database is not exhaustive and does not list awards and prizes that are offered and administered by music colleges, nor awards, grants and loans that may be available from local authorities.

Schools Music Association Founder's Fund

(www.schoolsmusic.org.uk)

The SMA Founder's Fund offers a limited number of small grants to young people up to the age of 18 who are in full-time education and suffering from financial difficulty. Grants are made to assist with the purchase of music or a musical instrument, or with the cost of attending a one-off event such as a summer music school. Ongoing courses cannot be funded, and priority is given to applicants who are supported by a member of the Schools Music Association, i.e. teacher, school/college, music centre, local SMA or LEA in membership.

Performance opportunities

National Association of Youth Orchestras

(www.nayo.org.uk)

The National Association of Youth Orchestras was formed in 1961 in order to represent youth orchestras throughout the UK and to foster their development. Its membership is open to all such organisations including student orchestras, chamber orchestras, symphonic, wind and jazz orchestras, and chamber music ensembles, whether independent or under the control of local authorities or music services. The Association continues to evolve in response to the needs of its members and represents a wealth of knowledge and experience gained over the years and available to its members.

BBC Young Musician of the Year competition

(www.bbc.co.uk/youngmusician)

BBC Young Musician of the Year is a biennial competition for outstanding instrumentalists. Applicants must be British, aged 19 or under and be of at least Grade 8 standard or equivalent. There is a £2,000 prize for each concerto finalist and a BBC Young Musician Travel Award for the winner.

National Youth Orchestra of Great Britain

(www.nyo.org.uk)

The National Youth Orchestra is one of the world's finest youth orchestras, which draws together each year over 150 talented musicians, aged between 13 and 19 years, from all over the UK. Each member of the orchestra has one thing in common – a passion and commitment to the study and performance of great music. The orchestra meets during the school holidays at New Year, Easter and in the summer for intensive two-week periods of coaching and rehearsal with NYO professors – leading professional musicians and teachers – and some of the world's finest conductors and soloists.

National Children's Orchestra

(nco-gb.org.uk/phpws)

The National Children's Orchestra has five age-banded orchestras, for children between the ages of 7 and 13 years. It draws together each year almost 500 talented musicians, divided into the five age-banded orchestras, from all over the UK. Their eldest group – the 'Main Orchestra' – is one of the world's finest children's orchestras. The NCO gives talented children the chance to play in a full symphony orchestra. The NCO's week-long residential courses are stimulating, educational and great fun.

Composing opportunities

dbass

(www.dbass.org)

dbass is the international educational resource for young people to connect, publish and share their original music. Whether your pupils are interested in creating music, publishing, or marketing and promoting, dbass allows them to develop skills in accordance with their strengths and apply them to a real life situation with a global audience. dbass believes in giving pupils a safe place to work and collaborate within.

All members must be part of an educational establishment and approved publishers monitor all content before it goes live to the internet.

Sound Inventors

(www.spnm.org.uk/?page=activities/soundInventors)

Sound Inventors is an award-winning programme of composition projects for young people aged between 12 and 18 years. Led and inspired by leading UK composers and musicians, it takes place in locations across the UK and enables participants to get to grips with writing and devising their own music. So far over 600 young people have worked with Sound Inventors teams to create and notate music in a variety of styles for performance by professional musicians.

Sonic Arts Network and Sonic Postcards

(www.sonicartsnetwork.org and www.sonicpostcards.org)

Sonic Arts Network is a national organisation working exclusively with sound and technology in creative, innovative and experimental ways. Sonic Postcards is concerned with the impact of sound on our lives and as with an ordinary postcard it offers the opportunity for people to exchange information about their local environments with a view to providing windows into a variety of other places, lives and cultures. The project is aimed at young people in primary and secondary schools aged between 9 and 14 years and their teachers, and is free to participating schools.

Make It Break It

(www.makeitbreakit.org)

Make It Break It is the scheme to enter if you want to get your music and media ideas in front of the people that matter and make decisions in the music business. It is a unique annual songwriting and enterprise awards scheme aimed at encouraging and uncovering fresh new talent from young artists and entrepreneurs. The judging panel includes Radio One DJs Mark and Lard, Coldplay's Chris Martin, Harvey Goldsmith, Steve Levine and various record and publishing industry executives. It is sponsored and run by Yamaha Kemble.

Specialist music schools

Specialist Schools Trust music colleges

(www.schoolsnetwork.org.uk)

There are currently 25 specialist music colleges, including five that combine music with another specialism and five that have music as their second specialism. Schools have been able to bid for music college status from October 2003. Each designated music college has its own distinctive ethos, but works towards the aims outlined in the music college mission statement.

Chetham's School of Music

(www.chethams.com)

Located in the heart of Manchester, Chetham's is a specialist co-educational independent school at the forefront of music education in the UK and abroad. Chetham's is open to all, irrespective of financial or social background. All UK entrants are entitled to government funding through the Department for Education and Skills Music and Dance Scheme, and there are generous bursaries available for overseas students. Entry to Chetham's is solely through musical audition; however, the school is one of the highest-ranked independent schools for GCSE and A level results.

The Purcell School

(www.purcell-school.org)

The Purcell School is one of the country's leading specialist music schools. Recipient of the Mozart Gold Medal awarded by UNESCO for its outstanding contribution to arts education, it enjoys an international reputation for excellence. Located near London, the Purcell School will provide inspiration and flexibility to fire the imagination and sharpen the skills of its gifted pupils. Above all, it offers the opportunity to work and perform with pupils of similar calibre.

Yehudi Menuhin School

(www.yehudimenuhinschool.co.uk)

Yehudi Menuhin founded this famous school in 1963 and created the ideal conditions in which musically gifted children might develop their potential to the full on stringed instruments and piano. Since 1963 the School has expanded and now educates more than fifty talented boys and girls between 8 and 18. In 1973 the School was accorded special status as a Centre of Excellence for the Performing Arts. Since 1975 pupils at the school have been funded by the Department for Education and parents only pay a contribution to the cost of their child's education according to their means. It is intended that children should be able to attend the school, once selected for their exceptional musical ability, whatever their parents' financial background.

And finally . . .

Help for parents from the BBC

(www.bbc.co.uk/music/parents)

The BBC has provided a lot of helpful advice here for parents about all aspects of music including musical games to do with young children, advice on learning instruments as well as interviews and careers advice from a range of celebrities and other musicians.

Conclusion

Look again at the practical context of music education. Increasingly, it is fed by music knowledge generated beyond school boundaries – in fact, on the fringes of the formal curriculum. Music knowledge is no longer produced solely in traditional scholastic haunts – university rooms, concert halls, conservatoires, music clubs and instrumental teachers. Rather it is in the hands of a diverse cottage industry of community musicians, orchestral and operatic 'outreachers', private music consultants, philanthropic professionals, the music nobility and pop stars – all of whom have their own way of approaching schools and curriculum. The boundaries of education spread far wider than the physical boundaries of the school, these days more than ever perhaps. Correspondingly, the knowledge base of music is changing, and is changing music education, while the music curriculum itself is frozen in legal aspic.

(Kushner 1999: 214)

As teachers develop new music education networks there are bound to be problems. We can all appreciate the many conceptual and practical difficulties that might occur as we seek to work collaboratively with other musicians. But, ultimately, we have to believe that they will result in the development of authentic and educationally worthwhile musical experiences for our pupils. Some may even reach the level of a crystallising experience that encourages and motivates a young person throughout the rest of their life. Of course, the quality of these experiences is partly dependent on the depth of musical understanding exhibited by project leaders. This may well be higher amongst insiders to a particular way of music-making. But, as teachers, we have a crucial role in maintaining a high standard of music education and ensuring that music teaching and learning within these new networks remains true to our core values and practices.

There can be little doubt that the knowledge base of music is changing and this has consequences for all of us as music educators. New ways of knowing will demand new ways of teaching and learning; standing still is not an option. Music, as we know, is a vehicle for the expression of humanity; people are not solely there as the vehicle for the music. Ultimately, the best education that a musically talented pupil can receive will be grounded in solid professional relationships with an individual teacher or group of teachers. Policy is undoubtedly important, but artistry and skill in teaching is a prerequisite to developing and promoting musical skill and understanding. Ongoing professional engagement with issues and ideas will ensure that we remain motivated, unhappy to settle with second-best and responsive to change. But, finally, it all comes down to the individual care and attention that all pupils need. And music is a wonderful medium within which our humanness can shine:

The more we talk with children and teachers the more music becomes entangled in lives and the more its significance fades in the light of experience. The closer we look at music events in schools the more we see that music is the pretext – life is the text.

(Kushner 1999: 216)

Appendices

Appendix 1.1
Ofsted – Expectations of schools in relation to able pupils

Appendix 1.2
National quality standards in gifted and talented eduction

Appendix 2.1
Free music resource websites

Appendix 2.2
A week in the life of a Year 10 musically talented pupil

Appendix 2.3
Sample form for documenting musically talented pupils' abilities

Appendix 4.1
Supplementary learning objectives from two QCA schemes of work for Years 7 and 9

Appendix 4.2
Dunwich Revisited – sound generation sheet

Ofsted – Expectations of schools in relation to able pupils

Evaluation focus	Issue	Judgement/evidence
Effectiveness of school	Inclusion/equal opportunities	● High achievement is determined by 'the school's commitment to inclusion and the steps it takes to ensure that *every* pupil does as well as possible.' (p. 25) ● At the parents' meeting, inspectors should find out if, in the view of parents, 'their children are progressing as well as they could; their children are happy in school, well taught and well cared for; the extent to which the school promotes equality of opportunity between different groups and includes *all* pupils and parents.' (p. 38)
Standards achieved by pupils	Achievement and underachievement	● Inspectors are asked to look at the achievement of different groups. (p. 44) ● 'If they (pupils) are readily capable of work beyond that which they are doing, they are underachieving.' (p. 45) ● A school should know 'how well gifted and talented pupils do and, where appropriate, how well pupils do in the school's specialist subjects ... Inspectors should judge how well the school uses information to identify and deal with underachievement, challenge the most capable and raise standards for all pupils.' (p. 48)
	Early entry	● Inspectors should be aware of special circumstances, such as 'a school policy on early entry for GCSE for some pupils.' ● 'Where pupils are entered early for GCSE examinations, inspectors should take account of the results in reaching a judgement about the performance of the year group as a whole and consider what early entry has allowed the pupils to achieve subsequently.' (p. 47)
	Discussion with pupils	● Inspectors should 'talk to pupils of different ages and levels of attainment (including) ... the high achievers.' (p. 54)
	Assessment	● Assessment might guide planning through 'review of pupils' progress, including whether targets have been met at the end of a unit of work to inform teaching and target-setting for the whole class, groups and individuals.' (p. 88) ● Inspectors should observe 'how targets for individual pupils of all abilities are agreed ...' (p. 88) ● Inspectors should take samples of students' work to see 'how assessment contributes to planning work for gifted and talented pupils ... and how the outcomes are considered in reviews.' (p. 88)

Evaluation focus	Issue	Judgement/evidence
Quality of education	Teachers' command of subject	• 'Pupils should be learning from experts.' • 'Teachers' knowledge is demonstrated in the way they . . . cater for the more able in a subject.' (p. 77)
	Appropriate challenge	• 'Effective teaching extends pupils intellectually, creatively and physically. Inspectors should judge whether teachers are determined to get the best out of the pupils and if they are being challenged enough.' (p. 78) • Inspectors are advised to 'observe what is done to challenge the most able pupils in the class, including those who may be identified by the school as gifted and talented. Watch for those pupils who are clearly not being challenged enough. What is the effect of lack of challenge on them? Where no obvious special provision is being made, find out why.' (p. 81)
	Learning methods and resources	• Judge the approaches used for pupils of high ability' (p. 79) • Inspectors should assess whether 'teachers involve all pupils in lessons, giving the diffident and the slower learners a chance to contribute and time to answer questions, and yet challenging the most able.' (p. 75)
	Homework	• 'How well is homework tailored to individual needs and capabilities?' (p. 81)
	Equality of access (to the curriculum)	• 'Does it take account of their cultural background and religious beliefs, diverse ethnic backgrounds, special educational needs and particular gifts or talents?' (p. 100)
	Pupil care	• Evidence of the care of pupils will include provision for those who are gifted and talented. (p. 109)
Management	Inclusion	• Does the school provide successfully for pupils who . . . are gifted and talented?' (p. 144)
Schools causing concern	Underachieving schools	• 'Triggers that might suggest a school is underachieving include: . . . lack of challenge and slow progress for particular groups of pupils (for example the most able), in certain classes, a particular stage or in several subjects.' (p. 164)
Initiatives for raising achievement	Excellence in Cities	• 'Gifted and Talented pupils should be identified in EiC schools . . . The school should have a policy and teaching programme for these pupils. Inspectors should evaluate the effectiveness of the school's strategy in motivating gifted and talented pupils and ensuring that they achieve as well as they can both in lessons and extracurricular activities.' (p. 30)

The page numbers refer to the Ofsted *Handbook for Inspecting Secondary Schools* (2003).

 From *Meeting the Needs of Your Most Able Pupils: Music*, David Fulton Publishers 2006

National quality standards in gifted and talented education

A – Effective teaching and learning strategies

Generic Elements	Entry	Developing	Exemplary
1. Identification	i. The school/college has learning conditions and systems to identify gifted and talented pupils in all year groups and an agreed definition and shared understanding of the meaning of 'gifted and talented' within its own, local and national contexts	i. Individual pupils are screened annually against clear criteria at school/college and subject/topic level	i. **Multiple criteria and sources of evidence** are used to identify gifts and talents, including through the use of a broad range of quantitative and qualitative data
	ii. An **accurate record** of the identified gifted and talented population is kept and updated.	ii. The record is used to identify under-achievement and **exceptional achievement** (both within and outside the population) and to track/review pupil **progress**	ii. The record is supported by a comprehensive monitoring, progress planning and reporting system which all staff regularly share and contribute to
	iii. The identified gifted and talented population broadly reflects the school/college's **social and economic composition,** gender and ethnicity	iii. **Identification** systems address issues of **multiple exceptionality** (pupils with specific gifts/talents and special educational needs)	iii. **Identification** processes are regularly reviewed and refreshed in the light of pupil performance and value-added data. The gifted and talented population is fully repre-sentative of the school/college's population
Evidence			
Next steps			
2. Effective provision in the classroom	i. The school/college addresses the different needs of the gifted and talented population by providing a stimulating learning environment and by extending the teaching repertoire	i. Teaching and learning strategies are diverse and flexible, meeting the needs of distinct pupil groups within the gifted and talented population (e.g. able underachievers, exceptionally able)	i. The school/college has established a range of methods to find out what works best in the classroom, and shares this within the school/college and with other schools and colleges
	ii. Teaching and learning is differentiated and delivered through both individual and group activities	ii. A range of challenging learning and teaching strategies is evident in lesson planning and delivery. **Independent learning** skills are developed.	ii. Teaching and learning are suitably challenging and varied, incorporating the **breadth, depth** and **pace** required to progress high achievement. Pupils routinely work independently and self-reliantly

	iii. Opportunities exist to extend learning through **new technologies**	iii. The use of **new technologies** across the curriculum is focused on **personalised learning** needs	iii. The innovative use of **new technologies** raises the achievement and motivation of gifted and talented pupils
Evidence			
Next steps			
3. Standards	i. Levels of **attainment** and **achievement** for gifted and talented pupils are comparatively high in relation to the rest of the school/college population and are in line with those of similar pupils in similar schools/colleges	i. Levels of **attainment** and **achievement** for gifted and talented pupils are broadly consistent across the gifted and talented population and above those of similar pupils in similar schools/colleges	i. Levels of **attainment** and **achievement** for gifted and talented pupils indicate sustainability over time and are well above those of similar pupils in similar schools/colleges
	ii. Self-evaluation indicates that gifted and talented provision is satisfactory	ii. Self-evaluation indicates that gifted and talented provision is good	ii. Self-evaluation indicates that gifted and talented provision is very good or excellent
	iii. Schools/colleges gifted and talented education programmes are explicitly linked to the achievement of SMART outcomes and these highlight improvements in pupils' attainment and achievement		
Evidence			
Next steps			

B – Enabling curriculum entitlement and choice

4. Enabling curriculum entitlement and choice	i. Curriculum organisation is flexible, with opportunities for enrichment and increasing subject/topic choice. Pupils are provided with support and guidance in making choices	i. The curriculum offers opportunities and guidance to pupils which enable them to work beyond their age and/or phase, and across subjects or topics, according to their aptitudes and interests	i. The curriculum offers **personalised learning pathways** for pupils which maximise individual **potential**, retain flexibility of future choices, extend well beyond test/examination requirements and result in sustained impact on pupil **attainment and achievement**
Evidence			
Next steps			

Definitions for words and phrases in bold are provided in the glossary in the Quality Standards *User Guide*, available at www2.teachernet.gov.uk/gat.

Generic Elements		Entry	Developing	Exemplary
		C – Assessment for learning		
5. Assessment for learning	i.	Processes of data analysis and pupil assessment are employed throughout the school/college to plan learning for gifted and talented pupils	i. Routine progress reviews, using both qualitative and quantitative data, make effective use of prior, predictive and value-added **attainment** data to plan for progression in pupils' learning	i. **Assessment data** are used by teachers and across the school/college//college to ensure challenge and sustained progression in individual pupils' learning
	ii.	Dialogue with pupils provides focused feedback which is used to plan future learning	ii. Systematic oral and written feedback helps pupils to set challenging curricular targets	ii. Formative assessment and individual target-setting combine to maximise and celebrate pupils' achievements
	iii.	Self and peer assessment, based on clear understanding of criteria, are used to increase pupils' responsibility for learning	iii. Pupils reflect on their own skill development and are involved in the design of their own targets and tasks	iii. Classroom practice regularly requires pupils to reflect on their own **progress** against targets, and engage in the direction of their own learning
Evidence				
Next steps				
6. Transfer and transition	i.	Shared processes, using agreed criteria, are in place to ensure the productive transfer of information from one setting to another (i.e. from class to class, year to year and school/college to school/college)	i. Transfer information concerning gifted and talented pupils, including parental input, informs targets for pupils to ensure **progress** in learning. Particular attention is given to including new admissions	i. Transfer data concerning gifted and talented pupils are used to inform planning of teaching and learning at subject/aspect/topic and individual pupil level, and to ensure progression according to ability rather than age or phase
Evidence				
Next steps				
		D – School/College organisation		
7. Leadership	i.	A named member of the governing body, senior management team and the lead professional responsible for gifted and talented education have clearly directed responsibilities for motivating and driving gifted and talented provision. The head teacher actively champions gifted and talented provision	i. **Responsibility** for gifted and talented provision is **distributed**, and evaluation of its impact shared, at all levels in the school/college. Staff subscribe to policy at all levels. Governors play a significant supportive and evaluative role	i. Organisational structures, communication channels and the deployment of staff (e.g. workforce remodelling) are flexible and creative in supporting the delivery of **personalised learning**. Governors take a lead in celebrating achievements of gifted and talented pupils
Evidence				

8. Policy	i. The gifted and talented policy is integral to the school/college's inclusion agenda and approach to personalised learning, feeds into and from the single school/college improvement plan and is consistent with other policies	i. The policy directs and reflects best practice in the school/college, is regularly reviewed and is clearly linked to other policy documentation	i. The policy includes input from the whole school/college community and is regularly refreshed in the light of innovative national and international practice
Evidence			
Next steps			
9. School/College ethos and pastoral care	i. The school/college sets high expectations, recognises achievement and celebrates the successes of all its pupils	i. The school/college fosters an environment which promotes positive behaviour for learning. Pupils are listened to and their views taken into account.	i. An ethos of ambition and achievement is agreed and shared by the whole school/college community. Success across a wide range of abilities is celebrated
	ii. The school/college identifies and addresses the particular social and emotional needs of gifted and talented pupils in consultation with pupils, parents and carers	ii. Strategies exist to counteract bullying and any adverse effects of social and curriculum pressures. Specific support for able underachievers and pupils from different cultures and social backgrounds is available and accessible	ii. The school/college places equal emphasis on high achievement and emotional well-being, underpinned by programmes of support personalised to the needs of gifted and talented pupils. There are opportunities for pupils to use their gifts to benefit other pupils and the wider community
Evidence			
Next steps			
10. Staff development	i. Staff have received professional development in meeting the needs of gifted and talented pupils	i. The induction programme for new staff addresses gifted and talented issues, both at whole school/college and specific subject/aspect level	i. There is **ongoing audit of staff needs** and an appropriate range of professional development in gifted and talented education. Professional development is informed by research and collaboration within and beyond the school/college

Definitions for words and phrases in bold are provided in the glossary in the Quality Standards *User Guide*, available at www2.teachernet.gov.uk/gat.
© Crown copyright 2005

Generic Elements	Entry	Developing	Exemplary
	ii. The lead professional responsible for gifted and talented education has received appropriate professional development	ii. Subject/aspect and phase leaders have received specific professional development in meeting the needs of gifted and talented pupils	ii. Priorities for the development of gifted and talented provision are included within a professional development entitlement for all staff and are monitored through performance management processes
Evidence			
Next steps			
11. Resources	i. Provision for gifted and talented pupils is supported by appropriate budgets and resources	i. Allocated resources include school/college based and nationally available resources, and these have a significant and measurable impact on the progress that pupils make and their attitudes to learning	i. Resources are used to stimulate innovative and experimental practice, which is shared throughout the school/college and which are regularly reviewed for impact and best value
Evidence			
Next steps			
12. Monitoring and evaluation	i. **Subject and phase audits** focus on the quality of teaching and learning for gifted and talented pupils. Whole school/college targets are set using prior **attainment** data	i. Performance against targets (including at pupil level) is regularly reviewed. Targets include qualitative pastoral and curriculum outcomes as well as numerical data	i. Performance against targets is rigorously evaluated against clear criteria. Qualitative and quantitative outcomes inform whole school/college self-evaluation processes
	ii. Elements of provision are planned against clear objectives within effective whole-school self-evaluation processes	ii. All elements, including non-academic aspects of gifted and talented provision are planned to clear objectives and are subjected to detailed evaluation	ii. The school/college examines and challenges its own provision to inform development of further experimental and innovative practice in collaboration with other schools/colleges
Evidence			
Next steps			

E – Strong partnerships beyond the school

13. Engaging with the community, families and beyond	i. Parents/carers are aware of the school's/college's policy on gifted and talented provision, contribute to its **identification** processes and are kept informed of developments in gifted and talented provision, including through the School Profile	i. Progression of gifted and talented pupils is enhanced by home-school/college partnerships. There are strategies to engage and support hard-to-reach parents/carers	i. Parents/carers are actively engaged in extending provision. Support for gifted and talented provision is integrated with other children's services (e.g. Sure Start, EAL, traveller, refugee, **LAC** Services)
	ii. The school/college shares good practice and has some collaborative provision with other schools, colleges and the wider community	ii. A coherent strategy for networking with other schools, colleges and local community organisations extends and enriches provision	ii. There is strong emphasis on collaborative and innovative working with other schools/colleges which impacts on quality of provision locally, regionally and nationally
Evidence			
Next steps			
14. Learning beyond the classroom	i. There are opportunities for pupils to learn beyond the school/college day and site (extended hours and out-of-school activities)	i. A coherent programme of enrichment and extension activities (through extended hours and out-of-school activities) complements teaching and learning and helps identify pupils' latent gifts and talents	i. Innovative models of learning beyond the classroom are developed in collaboration with local and national schools/colleges to further enhance teaching and learning
	ii. Pupils participate in dedicated gifted and talented activities (e.g. summer schools) and their participation is recorded	ii. Local and national provision helps meet individual pupils' learning needs e.g. NAGTY membership, accessing outreach, local enrichment programmes	ii. Coherent strategies are used to direct and develop individual expert performance via external agencies e.g. HE/FE links, online support, and local/regional/national programmes
Evidence			
Next steps			

Definitions for words and phrases in bold are provided in the glossary in the Quality Standards *User Guide*, available at www2.teachernet.gov.uk/gat.

Free music resource websites

ABC Music Notes (www.abcmusicnotes.com)

BECTA Music Advice (schools.becta.org.uk)

Birmingham Grid for Learning Music Resources (www.bgfl.org/bgfl/index. cfm?s=1&m=239&p=167,index)

California Association for Music Education, CMEA Bay Section (the website at www.cmeabaysection.org/resources.html provides an extensive list of music education resources)

Children's Music Portal (www.childrens-music.org)

Hampshire Music Service (www.hants.gov.uk/education/hms)

MMU Music Materials (www.jsavage.org.uk)

Musiced (www.musiced.co.uk/musiced.html)

Music Education Madness (American site) (www.musiceducationmadness.com)

Music 4 Education (www.music4education.com)

Music 4 Teachers (www.m4t.org)

Music at School (www.musicatschool.co.uk)

Musicland (www.themusicland.co.uk)

Musicwing (www.musicwing.com)

Music Teachers Resource Site (www.mtrs.co.uk)

Staffordshire Music Pages (www.sln.org.uk/music)

Teachernet (www.teachernet.gov.uk/teachingandlearning/subjects/music)

Trev's Music Education Pages (www.bumpmusic.co.uk)

A week in the life of a Year 10 musically talented pupil

Tuesday 10 May

Woke up to alarm on phone (*Gymnopédie No. 1*) and listened to music on the radio whilst getting ready. I usually listen to Key 103 or Radio 1 because they play a larger variety of music; I'm not into just one genre of music. Had a quick play of the piano before I left for school (probably about 8 bars of *Take Five*). Showed Rosie and Charlotte my two new ringtones – Oasis *She's Electric* and Aerosmith *Walk This Way*.

Unit 2 was the first lesson of music of the week. We continued listening and contributing to people's 'Guess Who's Coming to Dinner' – asking questions to the class about the Baroque period, involving Bach and Handel, the two biggest composers in this era. We also did more of the talks involving dance music and I really liked some of the songs people had chosen to discuss as I hadn't heard them for ages, e.g. Spandau Ballet *True* and Franz Ferdinand *Take Me Out*.

When I got home I played my scales. I am currently learning for my Grade 8 piano exam and played through two of the exam pieces, though I'm still at the sight-reading stage with one of them. Also played *Passigio, Einaudi, Flower Duet, Gymnopédie No. 1* and *Those Magic Changes* from the *Grease* soundtrack, amongst others. After this I watched music channels on TV (some good songs were on). At 6.30 I had my piano lesson and played through the pieces, scales, etc. Later I did my English coursework whilst listening to music on the computer, mainly The Killers, Lemar and Green Day.

Wednesday 11 May

Listened to radio in the morning: Key 103.

Also listened to a CD: Blur's Greatest Hits.

Had music lesson at school We continued with our talks and have now finished them but there are a few 'Guess Who's Coming to Dinner's to do on Friday.

After school I did concert band (playing my alto saxophone). We played *The Way You Move, Jungle Boogie, There You'll Be* and *One Day I'll Fly Away*.

Watched music channels at home but there weren't many good songs on.

Later found that Mum had bought the Razorlight album that I've wanted to get for ages. They're a new indie band who have released a new song – not originally on the album – called *Somewhere Else*. Other good songs include *Golden Touch* and *Up All Night*. I played the whole album.

Listened to the radio before going to bed.

Thursday 12 May

Woke up and listened to Classic FM in the shower (shower radio) and listened to Radio 1 in the morning whilst getting ready. Some songs that came on that I enjoyed were The Coral *In the Morning* and Razorlight *Somewhere Else*.

Flicked through the music channels when I got home but there was only rap on such as 50 Cent (who I hate) and Eminem. I like some rap, particularly Kanye West; Eminem is OK.

Surfed the internet later and listened to music (Brian McFadden, The Killers, Michael Jackson). I went on The Killers' website and read the Bolton Wanderer's website because I'm seeing Coldplay perform at their stadium (The Reebok).

Played some Ludovico Einaudi before bed, then listened to the radio – James Stannage on Key 103 (talk radio) and Tower FM (good for indie tunes).

Friday 13 May

Same routine as every morning except I listened to a CD – a mix including The Eurythmics (*Sweet Dreams*), The Beatles (*Michelle*), Extreme (*More Than Words*) and many others.

Listened to Rosie's iPod on the way to school. We listened to Kanye West and the Beatles (a bit of a contrast – my choice).

Got home and played *Rhapsody in Blue* on the piano.

Went to the Trafford Centre and listened to Razorlight there and back.

Watched Top of the Pops – Amerie, Oasis, Akon.

Stayed up later than usual and watched music channels. Songs that I watched/listened to were:

- Gwen Stefani *Hollaback Girl* ✓
- Akon *Lonely* ✗
- Black Eyed Peas *Don't Phunk With My Heart* ✓
- Nelly & Tim McGraw *Over and Over* ✓
- Coral *In the Morning* ✓

Saturday 14 May

Got up and watched Hit 40 UK on Popworld.

Got ready whilst listening to another mix CD – Brandy *What About Us*, Santana *Smooth*, Robbie Williams *Feel* and *Something Beautiful*.

Went to Manchester and bought the Tyler James single.

Listened to the radio before bed and played the piano.

Sunday 15 May

Read in bed whilst listening to the radio.

Listened to Classic FM in the shower, a Mozart concerto.

Went to Kathryn's and after watching a film we played on some guitars (she has about five). Kathryn taught me Nirvana *Come As You Are* which I can now play. She's not been playing for more than a few months but she can now play REM and a little Led Zepplin.

Practised saxophone. Played a little *Tin Root Blues* but mainly *Keepin' in the Groove* and *Blue Room*. They all involve improvising as well as a main motif/melody, but I focused mostly on the improvising as I'm weak at it.

Watched Indiana Jones on TV and really liked the music.

Monday 16 May

Listened to Radio 2 on the shower radio and Key 103 for about an hour in my room whilst getting ready.

Had my saxophone lesson at 1pm. Played *Take 5* and *Blue Room*. *Take 5* was a bit confusing because it was handwritten and in a new key – I was sight-reading it.

Did German coursework whilst listening to the Keane album on the computer. Songs they have released are *Bedshaped*, *This is the Last Time*, *Somewhere Only We Know*, *Bend and Break* and *Everybody's Changing*.

Listened to Athlete and U2 on the radio before bed. Both were new releases.

[Thanks to Ms Janet Redwood, head of music at Cheadle Hulme College, for organising the collation of this diary.]

 From *Meeting the Needs of Your Most Able Pupils: Music*, David Fulton Publishers 2006

Sample form for documenting musically talented pupils' abilities

Gifted and Talented Music Project nomination form
(produced by Emma Coulthard, Nottingham City LEA)

Child's name .... Age .... Class group ....

Class teacher ....

Please tick the statements that best apply to this child:

	Yes	No
Is captivated by sound	☐	☐
Often responds physically to music	☐	☐
Learns songs very quickly, often on first hearing	☐	☐
Sings or plays with expression and confidence	☐	☐
Makes music spontaneously, in or out of class	☐	☐
Selects an instrument with care and is unwilling to give it up	☐	☐

In general, this child:

Works well across the curriculum ☐   Works well in subjects
                                         that interest him/her ☐

Does not work well in class ☐

Prefers to work alone ☐   Prefers to be part of a group ☐

Works well alone and in groups ☐

Do you consider this child to be:

Very bright ☐   Bright ☐   Average ☐   Below average ☐

Any further comments or observations?

From *Meeting the Needs of Your Most Able Pupils: Music*, David Fulton Publishers 2006

Supplementary learning objectives from two QCA schemes of work for Years 7 and 9

Year 7: Form and structure (exploring structures)

Learning objectives Pupils will learn . . .	Activities	Learning outcomes
about structures and how they can help to organise sounds.	Discussion Structured listening Singing songs	Identify how structures can make it easier for the listener. Make sense of what is heard and remember musical material.
about call and response as a musical structure.	Performing a call-and-response song	Sing and accompany a call-and-response song with accuracy and appropriate dynamics. Comment on when and why the structure of call and response is used.
about ternary form as a musical structure.	Listening and analysing Singing or playing songs/melodies Structured composition Free composition	Sing and play music in ternary form, recognising when the first section is repeated by emphasising the beginning of the repeat. Compose music using ternary form, making contrasted sections with some musical links, e.g. rhythmic material.
about rondo form as a musical structure.	Class performance and composition Extended composition task	Recognise, describe and create pieces with contrasting sections in simple rondo form.
about structure as a way of organising musical material to create an intended effect; to use technical terms and everyday words that musicians use.	Paired compositions Comparative listening	Compose a 'journey', selecting appropriate structures to achieve intended effect. Make written notes to keep a record of ideas and experiments and use these to develop compositions. Collaborate with others to share information and ideas.

Year 9: Music and media (exploring how music is used)

Learning objectives Pupils will learn . . .	Activities	Learning outcomes
how music is used to create an intended effect.	Watching and listening Discussion	Identify when and how music is used to create an intended effect.
how music can convey different messages and emotions and specific intentions through a range of media.	Brainstorming and exploration Singing songs	Describe, using appropriate vocabulary, how and where different music can be used to portray specific and/or contrasting messages.
how a change of music can create a new effect in relation to other media.	Demonstration Example material and discussion	Recognise the relationship between musical features and the effects created, referring to specific musical devices.
about the ways in which music can be used to create an effective representation of a particular product.	Discussion	Explain why a particular composition may have been chosen for a specific advertisement.
how music affects the way we interpret visual images.	Listening and discussion	Identify specific ways in which music and visual images can be brought together.
about the effect of musical devices (discord, resolution, major/minor, dynamics, timbre, texture).	Composition to a literary stimulus	Identify specific musical devices used to create different effects.
to plan and compose a short advertising campaign suitable for a radio broadcast, from a non-musical stimulus.	Group composition	Plan, organise and present a short, effective advertising campaign suitable for radio broadcast; discuss and evaluate conflicting evidence to arrive at a considered viewpoint.

© QCA 2005 (adapted from www.standards.dfes.gov.uk/schemes2/secondary_music)

 From *Meeting the Needs of Your Most Able Pupils: Music*, David Fulton Publishers 2006

Dunwich Revisited – sound generation sheet

You have a number of things to help you with this stage of the project:

1. Your notes from the listening lesson and subsequent homework.
2. The sheet of notes we compiled from our class discussion.
3. Your memory of Mr Challis's composition with its sounds, atmospheres and emotions.
4. The sound ideas sheet summarising the results of the homework task.
5. The thoughts and ideas of other classes doing the project on the display boards.

Your task is to begin to create appropriate sounds that could be used in the Dunwich piece to be performed at Snape on 7 March 2000. Basically, we need two types of sounds:

- sounds that can be used to represent the natural setting of Dunwich (prior to the town being established and after its gradual erosion)
- sounds that can be used to represent the hustle and bustle of a busy town, social interaction, etc.

We have four sources from which these sounds can be generated:

1. Traditional instruments
2. Voices
3. Recorded sounds from different environments
4. Computer-generated sounds.

In your groups:

1. Choose an idea for which you would like to try and produce a sound.
2. Experiment with your chosen sound sources (instruments, voices, samples, etc.) and with any technology (sound processors, keyboard, computer, etc.).
3. Don't worry too much about the length of your sounds – short sounds can be repeated, longer sounds can be reduced in length if necessary.
4. When you are happy with the sounds being produced, document your work on a 'Planning Sheet' contained in the box at the front of the classroom. Fill this in very carefully, answering all the questions on the sheet in plenty of detail.
5. Be sure to think about the atmosphere, mood and emotion of the sounds being produced. There should always be a purpose for the type of sounds being produced.

Record your sounds on the Minidisc player and give the track a title (ask Mr Savage for help if required). Fill in the title of the track on the 'Planning Sheet' (this is vitally important).

 From *Meeting the Needs of Your Most Able Pupils: Music*, David Fulton Publishers 2006

References

Assessment Reform Group (2002) *Assessment for Learning: 10 Principles.* London: ARG.

Bernstein, B. (1971) 'On the classification and framing of knowledge' in Young, M. (ed.) *Knowledge and Control.* London: Macmillan.

Boden, M. A. (1990) *The Creative Mind: Myths and Mechanisms.* London: Weidenfeld and Nicolson.

Black, P. and Wiliam, D. (1998) *Inside the Black Box: Raising Standards through Classroom Assessment.* London: School of Education, King's College.

Black, P., Harrison, C., Lee, C., Marshall, B. and Wiliam, D. (2003) *Assessment for Learning: Putting it into Practice.* Maidenhead: Open University Press.

Bloom, B. S. (1956) *Taxonomy of Educational Objectives, Handbook I: The Cognitive Domain.* New York: David McKay Co. Inc.

Bruner, J. (1996) *The Culture of Education.* Cambridge MA. and London: Harvard University Press.

Cook, N. (1990) *Music, Imagination, and Culture.* Oxford: Clarendon Press.

Creative Partnerships (2005) *First Findings – Policy, Practice and Progress: A Review of Creative Learning 2002–2004.* London: Creative Partnerships.

Csikszentmihalyi, M. (1996) *Creativity: Flow and the Psychology of Discovery and Invention.* New York: HarperCollins.

Department for Education and Employment (DfEE) (1997) *Excellence in Schools.* London: DfEE.

Department for Education and Employment (DfEE) (1999) *National Curriculum for Music 2000.* London: DfEE.

Department for Education and Skills (DfES) (2002) *Training Materials for the Foundation Subjects.* London: DfES.

Department for Education and Skills (DfES) (2004) *Assessment for Learning: Guidance for Senior Leaders.* London: DfES.

Dust, K. (1999) 'Motive, Means and Opportunity'. *Creativity Research Review.* (www.nesta.org.uk/lowfat/kdust_rep.html)

Eisner, E. (2002) *The Arts and the Creation of Mind.* New Haven, CT, and London: Yale University Press.

Fautley, M. (2004) 'Teacher intervention strategies in the composing processes of lower secondary school students'. *International Journal of Music Education,* **22** (3), 201–18.

Freeman, J. (1998) *Educating the Very Able: Current International Research.* London: HMSO.

Gardner, H. (1983) *Frames of Mind.* London: Heinemann.

Gardner, H. (1999) *Intelligence Reframed: Multiple Intelligences for the 21st Century.* New York: Basic Books.

Green, L. (1988) *Music on Deaf Ears: Musical Meaning, Ideology and Education.* Manchester: Manchester University Press.

Green, L. (2001) *How Popular Musicians Learn: A Way Ahead for Music Education.* Aldershot: Ashgate.

Gregorc, A. F. (1979) 'Learning/teaching styles: their nature and effects' in Keefe, J. (ed.) *Student Learning Styles: Diagnosing and Prescribing Programs.* Reston VA: National Association of Secondary Schools Principals.

Hallam, R. (2000) 'Arts education in secondary schools: effects and effectiveness – a personal commentary with quotes from the full report'. (www.name.org.uk.)

Honey, P. and Mumford, A. (1986) *A Manual of Learning Styles.* Maidenhead: Peter Honey.

Honey, P. and Mumford, A. (1992) *The Manual of Learning Styles*, 3rd edn. Maidenhead: Peter Honey.

Jeffrey, B. and Craft, A. (2004) 'Teaching creatively and teaching for creativity: distinctions and relationships'. *Educational Studies,* 30 (1), 77–87.

Kolb, D. A. (1976) *The Learning Style Inventory: Technical Manual.* Boston MA: McBer.

Kolb, D. A. (1985) *Experiential Learning: Experience as the Source of Learning and Development.* Englewood Cliffs NJ: Prentice-Hall, Inc.

Kushner, S. (1999) 'Fringe benefits: music education out of the National Curriculum'. *Music Education Research,* 1 (2), 209–218.

MacDonald, R. A., Hargreaves, D. J. and Miell, D. (eds) (2002) *Musical Identities.* Oxford: Oxford University Press.

Mills, J. (2005) *Music in the School.* Oxford: Oxford University Press.

NACCCE (1999) *All Our Futures: Creativity, Culture and Education.* London: DfEE.

NACCCE (2000) *All Our Futures: Creativity, Culture and Education – A Summary.* London: National Campaign for the Arts.

NAME (2000) *Composing in the Classroom: The Creative Dream.* Matlock: NAME.

Neesom, A. (2000) *Report on Teachers' Perceptions of Formative Assessment.* London: QCA.

NfER (2000) 'Arts education in secondary schools: effects and effectiveness'. (www.nfer.ac.uk/publications/aries-data/arts-education-in-secondary-schools.cfm.)

Ofsted (2003a) *Handbook for Inspecting Secondary Schools.* London: Ofsted. (www.ofsted.gov.uk/publications/docs/hb2003/sechb03/hmi1360-01.html.)

Ofsted (2003b) *Inspection of Local Education Authorities; Ofsted/Audit Commission Inspection Guidance.* December 2003 v1a.

Ojumu, A. (2003) 'Total Respect'. *The Observer,* 21 October 2003, 48–49.

QCA (2005) 'Futures: meeting the challenge' (Forces for change, point 2). (www.qca.org.uk.)

Riding, R. J. and Rayner, S. (1998) *Cognitive Styles and Learning Strategies.* London: David Fulton.

Salter, J. (2005) 'Final word'. Association of Teachers and Lecturers, *Report* July/August, 30.

Savage, J. and Challis, M. (2001) 'Dunwich revisited: collaborative composition and performance with new technologies'. *British Journal of Music Education,* 18 (2), 139–149.

Savage, J. and Challis, M. (2002) 'A digital arts curriculum? Practical ways forward'. *Music Education Research,* **4** (1), 7–24.

Shepard, L. (2002) 'The role of assessment in a learning culture' in Desforges, C. and Fox, R. (eds) *Teaching and Learning.* Oxford: Blackwells.

Sternberg, R. and Davidson, J. (eds) (1986) *Conceptions of Giftedness.* New York: Cambridge University Press.

Swanwick, K. (1988) *Music, Mind and Education.* London: Routledge.

Swanwick, K. (1999) *Teaching Music Musically.* London: Routledge.

Van Tassell-Baska, J. (1998) *Excellence in Educating Gifted and Talented Learners,* 3rd edn. Denver CO: Love Publishing.

Wiggins, J. (2001) *Teaching for Musical Understanding.* New York: McGraw-Hill.

Wiggins, J. (2003) Handout from the East Anglian Researchers (EARS) meeting at Homerton College, University of Cambridge.